Sex Positions Guide

Tips and Techniques for Beginners to Explore Your Fantasies and Sexuality. Improve Your Sexual Life with Top Sex Positions and Spectacular Experiences for Couples, Women, and Men.

Scarlett Hunter

Table of Contents

Introduction

Congratulations on purchasing the book *Sex Positions Guide*, and thank you for doing so. You do not need to have a problem with your sex life in order to read this book, it is the perfect guide book for you to enable you and your sexual partner communicate better, understand on the importance of talking with each other about your sexual fantasies and desires; deepening the intimacy that you share, strengthen it, and appreciate how critical it is to recognize each other individually and as a couple.

The following chapters will address some of these issues, and of course, a whole lot more:

- You will get to know more about the importance of having intimacy in your relationship. But intimacy alone is not enough; you also need to add some romance and foreplay both in your love life and your sex life to have some genuine passion in your life.
- You will learn how easy it eases to strengthen the bond in your relationship, and this will translate to passionate lovemaking.

- You will get to know of a couple of techniques in the art of erotic massage and also how you can use sex toys properly to spice up your sex life.
- You will get to know more about sexual lubricants, and how to properly use them in a wide array of both solo and couple sexual encounters, and so much more.

There are plenty of books on this subject on the market, thanks again for choosing this one! Every effort was made to ensure it is full of as much useful information as possible, and please enjoy it!

Chapter 1: Intimacy, Romance, Foreplay

Intimacy

Relationships are solitary and desperate without affection to nurture love. In the highest sense, even between strangers, the stream of trust and respect between people should be intangible and yet tangible. I had encountered this, albeit seldom, often, as when a colleague revealed a section he was hidden for a long time.

Both of us committed to a deliberate, stable relationship, in which we would collaborate to share secret aspects of ourselves. He found the courage to ask me to sit down with him at the outset of our relationship so that he could inform me that which he had kept concealed within. We stood in the mid-summer sun in the afternoon under the grape arbor.

I could see in my hands, looking over him, how nervous he is, how difficult it was for him to ask me his most personal secrets. His body was rigid as he addressed the inner voices, which told him that openly revealing secrets was too dangerous, that if he did, it

3

would happen something wrong. He sat down on his chair edge, uncomfortably at first, facing me back with the sun.

I remember the unseen fingertips of my soul, reaching out to reach him as I saw him in pain. Everything my love and compassion for that guy have swelled me. I wrapped around him my heart-field and kept it as he started talking. He gradually started to relax his mind. It seemed as if some resistance flowed with every word he uttered from his body. He kept his head under pressure and then rested his arms. We held our hands on each other. I hugged all, breathing them in, and left a spot for them to lie down in me as the sounds and definitions of every phrase came up to meet me.

When he spoke, I quietly confessed to him with my head's regular nodes. My elbows rested on my arms, with my head in my palm. I bent back. Just for a few minutes, I knew he and I had traveled to some rare, other, and sacred land from the mundane world. We started to lose consciousness about the vibrations of the planet around us. The streams flow through the nearby river, and sometimes the car drives along the street, even the slight breeze in the woods. The heat of the sun spread from my skin's layer onto my bones ' eyes. My senses are strengthened. Colors also gleamed iridescently. I relaxed my eyes and became gentle and out of reach the harsh parts of the physical world, like the sides of a cotton ball.

My buddy and I expressed a mutual and secret awareness, without diverging from sharing his tale, that we had gone through an opening in the universe. When keeping the unknown world carefully, a little wild bee soared over and then halted. She hovered, seemingly touching, on the edge of us to taste the bond between us two.

She was floating, and then shifted from me to my brother, then suddenly, along the top, the bridge, of an invisible force field. The Bee would stop and taste this fantastic food like drinking in Nectar from a beautiful, unseen flora. As she was going from my buddy to me in a smooth line, she never adjusted her route. For a moment, in mid-air, she would stop near each one of us the way a dragon pauses momentarily in the air that is held by a string and air stretch before an invisible force changes its place.

The three of us were engulfed in an ecstatic, colorful universe at that time. The key to a gate was discovered, which had been closed until this time. We were in the world in which I was starving. So, I knew at that time that there is a planet behind us. The division of the two realms disappears through personal, profound connection and unity between hearts. I thought that all life responds as we do to love. And every day of my life, I needed that closeness, that light-world feeling as a way of life. It took me a while to reach the place where the two worlds are superimposed.

Food for The Soul of Love

When enough partnerships were boring, I felt empty and frustrated, and I knew that I had recognized the smell of discontent. I am thinking about something in my heart or something in my life. It's hard to know what came first, and it isn't essential in this case. It's critical that I went along.

The problem I revisited. Sitting in a café with a pen to a notebook, I put my heart and soul to the issue. "What's the depth for which I'm hungry?" Why is love not sufficient?" An authentic understanding of the world, as I read, came through my conscious mind, moved through my hands, out my ink, and exists on a page:" Intimacy is the nutrition that nourishes the heart of life. I continued to write to fill my mind and keep it in me. Love has a soul that needs care, nourishment, and nurture. The nutrition of love is a precious metal, a substance of life, which is selected every day and freely given as the newborn infant which wants milk suckling from the mothers ' breasts. When the baby exits the uterus, it moves into a new world. When we agree on the road of romance, we must flee the uterus of old familiar patterns that obstruct our affection. Security is our privilege to be raised.

Intimacy needs to take chances and go beyond the level of comfort. You must do what you are most scared of to attain a life of privacy. Private, sacred life calls for exposure and vulnerability. It needs to sensitize you to a range of sensations and emotions; in increasing elegance, from rough to subtle. The foundation from which love develops is to be together with what you hear.

You need to be able to run and lie down in the pit of yourself. It requires rigorous self-assessment (or self-diagnostic data from Star Trek) so that everybody present can see yourself. And it asks that through the eyes of wonder, you may see and marvel at the world.

There is no intimate relationship in which either party silences, loses, or betrays the other, and each party communicates in combination strength and insecurity, weakness, and talent. From early childhood, I accepted it on the grounds of my (at those times) conviction that there was not enough affection to go any direction so that somebody would get inadequate and break his heart. And I was scared that someone would think that something was very wrong with me or that I was not lovable if loves had been through, even if I had permission me to open up. For too long, there was too much danger that someone would figure this out. I built barriers that prevented it from moving far or so far as love began coming in the secret places within like water finding its way across sand, stone, and gorges.

I needed to break strong beliefs and behavior patterns to have the level of intimacy I desired. I started giving up ideas about who I was feeling. I gave up the love to be alone, to exclude, and to privatize my emotions. The substantial part of me, the hard part that people met first, I abandoned the façade of power I had crafted over the years. I've made this ability to watch my dad. This seemed like it succeeded for him, and a universe is a dangerous place, after all. I made a big part of it to mask how scared I am. But the deep gentle core inside me, my power protected. I kept my childlike natural self in a bag. I find not many people wanting to look beyond the delusions or the sadness to see the truth of who is hidden below when I give up these things. Ultimately, I had to renounce expecting others to be happy in the life that I knew I wanted to lead.

I discarded these things as they blocked, like razor wire, the road to what I needed most: friendship and independence. I desired, firstly, to be safe, genuinely free, the sort of freedom which comes only from awakeness, knowledge and obligation for my life; independence, born when I am present inside my body; freedom from personality strength; versatility of decisions, and being not the object of anything around me so that I can think. It was too overwhelming to be near that I gave up running, gave up building combat to the range. I wanted to do the stuff that frightened me the most. I choose anywhere. The degree of trust I would calculate could be shielded from the amount of fear I had. If I had tremendous energy, when I rattled and felt pressure, there was a suggestion that it was necessary to say something out loud, as I realized in my birth family at a young age that sound was not created and that I was invisible.

How many of us are doing this? Learn to keep quiet as the status quo is compromised for our fundamental desires and right to life?

Romance

Thirty years my parents have been married. Yet I figured we would not split with assurance. Not because they adored one another openly and gazed at one another with loving eyes, much the same. I just thought they'd live with each other indefinitely because other men, not my parents, had divorced. But it came in, and when I was 21, they split. I knew better, but I still fell into my room and gave him a good old scream.

To new boyfriends and wives, I couldn't picture my family, either. Great! Big! It made me sick to my stomach to know that I didn't feel anybody else. But after only a year of my parents "on the market," my mother called from her background with a fantastic story. This boy called Tom dated from when she was 15 to 20 years old. Tom's been her honeymoon high school. Both went to each other's proms and had images to show their development together during adolescence. You loved each other madly until one horrible day, my mother found in Tom's wallet a picture of a girl, not even a naked portfolio, and she was screaming out hell. It was just inside because the girl gave it to him and that's it Tom swore to my mom. Mom did not trust him and kicked him out. At all times, she was humiliated, and Tom stopped. Yet Tom never gave up. He pounded at the windows, arrived at her job, and attempted everything except to send Mom the gift box in with her shoes. Mom soon began to meet this man called Dan, who happens to be my uncle. He just came back from Vietnam and was a warm little cupcake after my mama. As my mother said, they hesitated until they had sex, so in a matter of months they agreed to click the nod. The engagement had been scheduled for a week. She was down; however; she was so right. That evening, Tom showed up and said, "Do not do it, please. Mother started popping the nose, and she said, "I'm so sorry, but my mother has already been saving for the marriage." Everyone screamed, but then she did what she had to do: she flung him away as quickly as she could. I love you, Linda, I am my soul. You marry the guy. She knew he was her life's love, but she couldn't do anything about it. Never again did they see each other. Ugh! Ugh! Ugh! It killed me. I couldn't believe my mother's heart was elsewhere for thirty years!

I began to be terrified when she finished telling me this story.

So romantic! Very sweet! I say that it was a bit upsetting the section about not wanting to marry my father, but it felt like the love of life. I told her we ought to try to find him–perhaps he was also divorced. Much of the baby boomers are single, and I figured their chances were pretty big.

"I have identified him," she responded. "My mother worked as a courthouse garrison to give you some history. Hey, a man. She had washed prison cells and toilets and had a great time serving. This is how, I guess, live saints roll.

Just the day before, she had cleaned up a courtroom, and a defendant left as he missed his lawsuit. It was Tom, and she looked up. Everyone glanced at one another for a second in silence. "Tom?" my mom asked."It was like a session between Luke and Laura, but without the male permissions at the General Hospital. We moved in surprise cautiously towards each other. He looked the same, she said, unless he was bearded. They spoke about how much time it took for them and compared their families ' notes. Instead my mother dropped the card "I'm separating" to see what he would do. I replied,' Dad, it's supposed to be. Tom said,'' I'm separated from my wife.' It's your life's passion! My mom replied, "Ok, I can't go for something until he's divorced." I begged her to go out for lunch, at least. I couldn't believe you guys find each other like this. She figured she should burn in hell anyhow for my father's divorce, so I replied, "Why don't be bad, because you're going there already?"She laughed, and I could hear an enthusiasm I had not heard in her voice in years.

Foreplay

That's why: let's imagine you were out with a girl, and now you have an excellent talk. You're back in your place. You're watching her over. She smiles at you. She looks back. You want to kiss her. You want to kiss her. She thinks you want to touch her. She understands.

You realize she's an influential person. And she could deny you permanently, should you try to kiss her and drag her back. Perhaps it will happen later, or it might also hug you if you don't try to kiss her. The threat of forever getting refused is so high that you are afraid that you "move ahead" and have faith that something will change sooner.

Or let's imagine you were out a couple of times with a girl, and for the first time, you just kissed her.

She loves it, you see. You like her, she understands. You would like to do more; however, you believe you will be seen to "move too quickly," or worse if you attempt. A "pervert pushy." after you have spent and come so far, you hate the idea of being refused. So, you choose to rest and hope things will "heat up" later.

If you stop and consider it, the reason for issues in such circumstances is that:

1) You don't know exactly what turns women on. We have all been there.
2) The dismissal is worrying you.
3) And you pause, you don't understand what she's doing.

I honestly believe that most people warn themselves when it comes to getting a woman with their dilemma and opposition. Yeah, that's wrong, you wrote. The men cause issues are the ones. This isn't the girlfriend! It's because you don't understand what's happening, what is happening, and how to continue.

Which people want... Why women need? But never will you be asked here's a little hidden that most people will never reveal. We know what's on your heart. They understand your thoughts. A woman will tell you who you feel! Who you think! If you want a touch, however secretly, you know that. Whether you love her and you want to do something, you realize. Because you learn. You understand.

This is the kicker: when you ask her to deny you, she knows. Females are around ten times good as men to understand, to perceive the secret language of the body, so we recognize what we are. I know what most men think. When you understand how and why a woman gets excited physically, then the changes, let's talk a bit about the resistance and rejection problems.

Here's an exciting thought: Albert and Elizabeth Allgeier note in their book "sexual interactions," that in one survey, almost 40 percent of women indicated that they rejected intercourse unless they desired it. You call it "no token." what is happening here? What is happening? Incidentally, I want to find out, before I address it, that this does not imply a woman wants a guy to impose on her. Do nothing to force a woman.

The anticipation of girls. Advancement adds to sexual excitement. Write it down. Write it down. On your front.-on Your front. You should recognize this girl, as the concept of wanting and expecting.

The explanation most women say they don't want to sleep with men is because the guy doesn't get it. Men are behaving like if a girl takes her clothes off and tells "let's do it." it is because a person doesn't have to do it.

A woman acts like a guy who needs them to be pursued all night long. And then you can do something. And then maybe. Yeah.

And if you want her to be more enticed and to have less "resistance," then I have a strategy I use, which is "two steps forward, one step back." I have a methodology I teach. This is a means of instilling the sexual excitement of a woman and of amplifying the lust already there.

That's how things function: let's pretend you speak to a lady and hold her hand in place. Take your hand back and stop after a couple of minutes.

Lean back. Lean back. Lean back. Continue to talk. A couple of minutes later, reach over again and hold her hand. And continue to speak. Turn to hug her now. Now. Stop, after hugging her.

Only lean back again. Lean back again. Continue to talk. A few minutes later, touch it and hug it once more.

Kiss her a little longer this time. A bit deeper, hug her. Enter, instead.

Lean back. Lean back. Lean back. Smile. Smile. Smile.

We with you? You were stunned when using this strategy. First and foremost, the situation is changing absolutely. Installing you in front of a female who fights you, she will most likely try to get you to do more.

So maybe I should ask him we're not going to sleep together this afternoon. But this is good. "and the best part of that technique's that it works you work to you! She wouldn't say of myself," oh, what's happening here? Some people try to push on me, but they don't do anything. They would never tell this to you. Even though she doesn't want to convince you a person could clarify, she wouldn't. Woman wants people that get everything.

Cuddling

I like cuddling myself. One night when I talked to a girl, I discovered something almost entirely by accident. We addressed the differences between men and women, and I said something in this regard: "Can you cuddle? If I had to choose between cuddling or sex, I'd always like to cuddle. Yeah, I would have to choose to cuddle. Don't get me wrong, and I love sex. But the best thing about cuddling. you can cuddle all night?"I said," I like kissing. I like kissing and cuddling. And all night, contact someone. She began to say, "Right now, I just turn on" by the time I was finished. Then she. She wanted me to have contact with her by phone, honestly!

Since then, I have had this occur many times on the phone, and this is not a mistake. If you communicate with a girl if you begin to talk about hug, cuddle, contact. And about it, you're descriptive. "I like to pass down your back the tips of my fingertips where your chest reaches" Generally, a person may begin to experience this.

So we go away from the cafe (because I asked you "Yeah, let's go.") and we are back at my place. We're going home from the coffee.

If it's in the evening, glance at your watch and suggests, "I gotta get up early in the morning. But. all right, you should go in for a couple of minutes." That's great! You -with her like she tries to persuade you to let her in, and she said nothing! Sweet. Nice. Nice. I walk in and let her follow her. (Read again, if you did not pick up what I said.) Ok, if you act chevalier and simultaneously breast their balls, you'll be rewarded with good things from Santa. (Once again, I always open doors for women, I walk outside the curb, and pull chairs out.)

So now I'm in the bedroom. And I'm bringing her on a ride. So either I'm lying on my bed and speaking to her, or I'm on the floor. And I get a bit calmer and let her talk as I watch her. I turn away and continue to search. Occasionally I look away like something.

Then, when she talks, I reach her and begin to stroke her hair. I first hit down on the ground. I consider the indication that she's in my bed WAAYYYYY and will likely want to have sex in 60 minutes if she's OK with this, (if you have any question, ask a lady if she's going to let a guy hit her hair on the bed for the first time if she's not inside it).

I used to do all sorts of acupuncture and other stuff, but now I'm using the easy hair stroke test. This is a perfect puzzle piece. If you like your hair stroked, Far LEAST is going to make it with me easily. I'm trying to do sometimes a hand rub here, or somewhat a little neck massage, but I'm dragging her next and cuddle her. And find the murderer.

I just liked the smell of the girl myself. And I started smelling her shoulders as she laid around me with my hair stroking. Just a little, then more, and more. Even her hair stroking.

I smell her neck and ears. I don't kiss, no tackle at all, in about five or ten minutes. Nothing! No! No! I smell, lean, and act like I enjoy feeling complete, and it is relaxing. Try my boys if you can still feel. You won't believe it, and she gets so turned up! She should try kiss me at some point. That's what I'm waiting for. I'm going to let her lips enter mine and just brushing a teensy bit. And then I'm going to go back and start to taste. I can tell,' Wow, you're ahead of us.'.. love it.

I will hug her after a few. Then run my hands through her eyes — all the sweet stuff to do. Then again, I will begin. I'll start again. This form of harassment is enjoyable for girls. I like it. You know it.

I'm waiting for her to do something personal. I am grinding her hips on me, for starters. Or hold my butt. And give. None. The woman usually does something subtly sexual, first when I'm patient. This is important, as it is the attacker. So I make a vocal pass to suggest,' You've got to do all it takes to say PLEASE.' It's okay, man. So she'll say for the first time, "No-no-no. And I'm just thinking, "Okay," I'm not going to beg you.

Then I'm turning over or lying down and look around. Outside of this. Typically, it leads the female to wonder what happens and come over and cuddle, hug, etc. me again.

I begin to breathe through her mouth, and I start to breathe. All these good things. All those good things. So I suggest, "All you need is to tell PLASSE." All right, you get the picture when you get to work up again, and I hear her pulse getting faster, heart rate rising, etc. I proceed to do so until it asks, "Yes, all right.

Your seven-step Physical Contact Guide

1) When you return to the building, suggest, "Yeah, I'm going to need to get up early in the morning. But. Okay, you're going to go in for some minutes."

2) Use The Kiss Test–Begin your hair while you speak. Use the Kiss Test! She's in you if she loves it!

3) Lean in her arms and feel soft. Pull back. And render it again. Work slowly to allow her chest and eyes to think.

4) Continue to build tension, give her finally a kiss, pull back then. Accus HER to "present."

5) Wait for her to make the first sexually aggressive pass. then suggest, "Just just say everything you have to do."

6) Once she replies, "Yes," turn over and look away, leaving her intrigued. Step back and wait before she comes to you.

7) Turn the heat up with the sensual touch, the air in its eyes, etc until it becomes more enthusiastic (i.e., moving harder, pounding in the chest, etc.).

Chapter 2: Sexual Communication and Erotic Massage

Sexual Communication

We see on the "big screen": two fans collapse in the water, waves roaring, corpses tied up. Everything so sexy and transparent! Everyone else has to struggle for encounters in actual bedrooms that aren't so sexy: small penises, weak desire, very early ejaculation, vaginal agony, and many more! You can't ignore those issues, but how do we talk? An erotic life is difficult, and it may be uncomfortable or frightful to think about it. Without the ability to communicate gender, a marriage would likely be detached, stressful, and even dull! Take a moment to explore a very private topic. Join us. Sex!-Sex!

A pair of Suzanne and Sam went to therapy to resolve their gender difference in their early 50s. Sam found that his sex drive was small, a shift for him. Suzanne frequently learns several nuances about herself and addresses the changes of menopause with her gynecologist. A vaginal hypothermic or hormone cream is prescribed by the nurse. The libido of Suzanne began to return, and it became more sexual. Sam admitted he had erectile changes, which were very disheartening. He was afraid of trying to communicate, finding that his erection was not as stable as it was when he was old. Sam and Suzanne were told by their psychologist about routine physical adjustments in men and women as they grew older. When they explored their shifting roles and desires and heard about it, Suzanne and Sam started to unwind in terms of performance goals. We noticed that it provided relaxation and a rekindled sexual relationship to speak frankly about the complexities of aging.

The Bridge to Sexual Awareness

They imagine the road for better communication around gender on a bridge. The trip starts with the desire to learn the extent of one's individuality. The route across the bridge comprises of many variables. Some refer to individual sexuality: perceptions of children's lives, sexual injuries, sexual uniqueness, and the challenges of life.

Others relate to a partner like communication, expectations, struggles with relationships, and desires. These personal components and interactions lead to sexual awareness. A person may allow him or her to have his or her sexual voice heard about these things.

The Need to Talk About Sex

There appears to be a lot of talks! Dr. Phil and Oprah do it. Books about it are available. What, then, is all this emphasis on speech? They realize as counselors that some individuals aren't comfortable talking.

Women in general! The social habits, lectures, and personal relationships were disrupted by pain. We know that many important things continue to simmer on the back of the bronze before things get to the point of boiling without someone raising the topic.

Sexual Healing

Why is it essential for me to get acquainted with gender? My sexual problems are not just my problem, and I don't think that it is our problem. My partner also has issues!

Before you can move on this information to someone else, you must learn yourself. If you talk about sex, it's useful if speaking to someone else to consider where their thoughts and assumptions come from. By understanding where you come from and where you plan to go, you cannot have a discussion. It's an "our" issue for a group. We understand. But first, you have to know yourself.

How to Talk About Sex

In a marriage, interaction is a crucial part of it. It is also essential to get nearer, feel safer, and establish greater trust through communicating ideas and feelings correctly and experiencing compassion. Responding with regard creates an environment in which freedom of expression occurs. Slowly begin intimate discussions, remember to maintain a sense of humor, and to be aware of positive and negative reactions. Bear in mind that a secure space is needed for gender conversations, and a marriage is not always a haven. To get to a place where there is security, some wounds from the past may have to be corrected. When you consider a physical or emotional intimacy uncomfortable, you might need professional help to improve empathy, to feel happier and to develop a more satisfying sexual partnership.

Clear contact with sexual needs, anxieties, and expectations should be encouraged. Be aware we will be moving slowly throughout this book and give some instances. It is safe to say that there are other fields of contact which also have issues with sexual communication. Communication encourages conversation, but it can seem like your companion talks a foreign language if you're unconnected. During their teens, Tyler and Tessa, a young couple, came to see a psychologist first with a few sentences. Tessa challenged Tyler to clarify why they had provided a service, so she went over her head, sitting and talking to her friend. Tyler became upset as he explained that for the two years of his marriage, he had been struggling with quick ejaculation. You could not talk about it at home without tears and struggles. Tyler blamed himself, and Tessa felt hopeless and angry. The sexual problems of Tessa and Tyler have permeated their marriage in another way. The stress of the ongoing sexual issue has contributed to conflicts between them when trying to talk about money and time management. As they did not feel that they were intimate partners in the house, also in the other facets of their marriage, they did not feel near and connected. Tessa and Tyler both hated the confrontations and started preventing time to talk, contact or schedule. They had been able to speak of their mutual issues after several months of practicing effective communication, which allowed them to become more related and comfortable.

Communication Tips with Your Partner

- Listening is a practical thing. Most of us find it challenging to understand the other party as we formulate our refutations.
- The gap is between you and your friend. Don't expect consensus. Don't anticipate compromise. Achieve inclusion. Expect complexity.
- It can make you feel better and stronger just by expressing your rage, yet it won't help the marriage. Try to speak, but be polite and not aggressive as well.
- Maintain to a minimum the claims. The data your mate can't keep to is so big. It's getting awful.
- If you need clarity, ask specific questions.
- Keep out of generalizations, saying, "You stay away. "And' You never.' You never Time-out is an excellent tool as long as you and your companion adhere to the guidelines and return later to the problem.
- Consider how to preserve private conversation. Is it all right to discuss your sexual issues with your best friend or brother?
- Seek to paraphrase the other person's words. Make sure that you always listen to your friends.
- Show concern for the emotions of your friend. Empathy indicates you don't comply with your

stance or view. Empathy demonstrates compassion, validation, and comprehension.

- Use the announcements, "I think." Don't think you know the mood of your friend. Stop the claims of "you."

- Lecture works at a state fair only! Take a look at each other's things. Mind you are not your partner's specialist.

The Brain's Role in Sex and Love

Despite differences in youth, singularity, and personal struggles, this book is aimed at helping people connect and think about sex. Yet our chemical composition, what? Apart from some variations in sex, they seem to be biologically very identical.

Why do we want physical comfort and love? To explain shifts in our sexual relationships, it helps to examine the ebb and flow of passion. Knowing the psychology of "lovemaking" will help us understand the intense emotional and sexual drive in long-term relationships.

Three separate systems seem to play a part in what is referred to as love. For general, testosterone for both men and women is the first processor motivation, desire. We are guided to search for sexual partners by hormones and chemicals in early brain structures.

The second method, romantic love, is explored in Helen Fisher's book Why We Love, which tells of experiments using neuro-imaging in brain-related chemicals1 in which a few people focus exclusively and intensely on each other, the phase of romantic love usually lasts around six to 18 months. Scanning using FMRI has shown that people looking at a photograph of their loved ones have decreased their behavior substantially in the brain area called the ventral tissues field. Their presence is defined as the ventral tissue zone. Cells in this region of the brain release dopamine, a neurotransmitter that causes us to look for meat, water, and gender, for instance, which are necessary for survival. Dopamine has been dispersed to numerous areas of the brain and helps us to focus on and concentrate on a goal, producing a lot of power and "feelings of pleasure." There is a sensation of intense, even massive, recognition, when the target of interest is identified, which motivates us to go on. The hormone testosterone is often driven up by dopamine and, therefore, longing for women.

The third system is called connection or corresponding love and consolidates the link. Neuroscience has shown to be increasingly active in this process and seems to be mostly stimulated by two receptors, oxytocin, and vasopressin, which are closely inundated in the brain. This response tends to affect dopamine and norepinephrine activity in the brain, which decreases the impact of romantic love and triggers an anticipation surge that first "harvested" to drop.

As described above, the romantic stage inevitably fades into any partnership. How often has this deep nasty feeling of "joy" driven company, only to find that it vanishes over time? It is normal that when we think sexual attraction is gone, we get depressed?

Sexercises

Take the connection with sexual consciousness, which we mentioned in this chapter earlier. Think whether each statement is correct or incorrect while reading the following comments.

- Human contact is helpful to me.
- My body makes me feel good.
- I have faith in my friend.
- I'm sure.
- I feel good about myself.
- My religion has sent me encouraging gender signals.
- I think the media shouldn't represent my sex life.
- I sound as though I am mindful of my physical injuries.

- The personal disorders (therapy or the partner) have been dealt with.
- I recognize that the personal expectations of my wife and I are different.
- I agree my mate may have different gender likes and dislikes.
- I know that my sex life has problems (aging, birth, disease, sexual disturbance, emotional difficulties, etc.)
- My wife and I effectively communicate on gender.
- I've got realistic sex standards.
- I know there's a lot of gender stereotypes.
- My wife and I can work in marriage combat (conflict, sex, energy battle, company, etc.).
- I know what's going on with me.
- I know what's going on with my wife.
- I am hunting for gender spicing.
- I frequently get hot dates from my wife and me.
- I can talk to my therapist easily about sex.
- I could speak to my healthcare provider quickly about gender.

You have taken the right book if you have replied "true" to some of those comments! Speak with your partner to make your guidelines, and you feel secure. You may want to talk outside your bedroom so that your bedroom is safe. Write down your journal rules, and each time you sit down to discuss gender, read each other, if appropriate. Take into account the safety and what you want. Every spouse should discuss with him or her what is healthy. Do you have to be reassured? Generally, you enter a point where you think that you are not understood when you have discussions? Which causes could affect your partner's listening? Where should the talks take place? Is there a problem with interruptions? Try to discuss how to end the debate, so no partner feels like it's unresolved.

Try to consider as many sexual terms as you can if both you and your wife are in the right place. In your journal, write down the terms. When you were a kid, think of what you considered your body bits, the amusing words you have learned during your lifespan as well as the medicinal terminology. Be sure that during this argument, you maintain your sense of humor!

Start talking daily about gender! Test schedule, concentrate on one question every week, like:

➢ What is a film with a sex scene that turned you on?
➢ Where is the right spot other than a bed for lovemaking?

- What are you've ever read the best pornographic story?
- What kind of music "inspires" you?
- Why did you think life would be before you got children?
- Recall trying to keep the sexual activity pleasant and enjoyable!

There will be time to talk about more serious issues, but the goal here is to get you and your wife to talk about sex. Stay away from things that are psychologically laden. One good idea is to write down the queries, may them in a bowl, and choose one every week to answer them. So you're always going to have to talk about something!

Erotic Massage

Saying "Absolutely" is a strength in our society that we have acquired. Entertainment is generally not placed on our schedule every day. "Sounds nice, but I don't have space." Sadly, we do not do fun well. We don't have room for enjoyment. During our everyday lives, how many of us are affected? We were carried, kissed, and stimulated the whole day when we were children. Do we feel we no longer need it as adults? Do we hide a grave famine in our activity to feel appreciated, appreciated, and wanted?

How can a hard worker, who is tired, become a restful, touch-fed person? Do we need instruction from a physician? "You're feeling bizarre; you're going to go home, languish in the arms of your loved one until revived." We all recall being "taken" for dreaming like a baby, and being reprimanded by a parent or teacher: "Quit day-dreaming; you're wasting time." But what was was was lost at that moment? "Sales are down: go back, take a more extended sensual bath, relax, and dream daytime.

Yet we do not seem to get around to being. We are a planet full of human characters. We're just human beings. And how much happiness just independence do we find through our frenetic activity and achievement?

Our anxious, dualistic mentality always drives us to believe that we have two sides to choose from. In this book, I want to tell you that between hard work existence and fun, you don't have to decide; instead, you can have both. Harmony enriches our worlds, and every day we celebrate the strength and happiness of our bodies.

Consent for Extra Pleasure

As a coach for sex and intimacy, my main task is to allow people to have more fun. I am an advocate for fun. "Choose nice, my mantras. Do this for you. Do it for you. Just have it your way. Have it your way. Say yes to wishes — please say it!" I encourage women to flirt, turn on, and praise. I help men turn off their rational minds to "go" to enjoy the moment and experience with their bodies. I see a smooth wash of my customers ' eyes, animation, and hope come and play for the overshadowed girl or boy. I saw it, and it's something I love watching.

A place of fun, I like to picture. "Want to talk about the biggest experience I had last night?" You invite a pal excitedly. And, when I was playing in the laundry room this morning, "the funniest thing happened." Or, teasingly, "Have I ever said about you my dream...?"They are all people. We are all hearing. We are core boys. They are girls. How long have we stopped playing? When are we able to begin again?

Erotic massage can lift the game limit for yourself. I recommend a regular dose of touch if you feel fatigued or repetition in your life–sensual, no stress, no-destination contact. I recommend you plan on exploring the erotic body with massage activities in the book for some time— five, ten, and 20 minutes most days (and occasionally for some more). Pleasure is a matter of course. Set it to the schedule.

The Electric Body and Breathing

The secret to an erotic massage is the practice of basic breathing strategies.

Conscious breathing helps you to liberate your friend from the chatter and the need to "perform." Breath consciousness may push erotic energy creates into an electrifying sensation of the whole body in an environment, like genitals.

Conscious breathing slows down the mind, deepens feelings, and suspends the average time. We may undergo a warm, healthy rebirth by concentrating on the respiratory system. Our perception of alienation disappears, and self-destruction evaporates, and we feel energized and comfortable at the same time. The way to connect with your companion and the entire universe is to concentrate on your heart.

In the West, they missed the sensibility of the wind that many cultures have long exercised as an accessible yet profound tool of personal transformation.

You might be shocked by how the ocean breathing exercises could bring about significant and dramatic improvements.

Solo Ocean Breathing

Ocean respiration is heavy, quick breathing, with "Ahhh" on the exhalation at times. If you offer and accept an erotic massage, it's a sure path towards sexual submission and trance. Practice sea breathing by slightly narrowing in the nose, so that you can hear the flow through your nose. Recall when you were a kid, and somebody put your head in a jar and said, "Hey, you hear the inside of the sea." This is the sound you make with every inhales through your nose. Let your calm stomach grow with the inhalation and let your mind track your breath's ocean echo into the heart.

On the expiration, open your mouth slightly and release an "Ahhhh" like fogging your wet, warm exhalation mirror. Remove the mouth to hear the sounds when sighing and moaning. Try to put your palm over your neck to sense the sensations. Let the noise stream through the open throat without effort.

Learn to "catch the wind" for each step by holding the air in and out of your head. Hide your stomach flat.

Keep your belly firm. Instruct your brain to track the rhythm of every step over and over again. Yogis know you're in the present moment when you can hear your breath and follow it. Practices of meditative or religious sexuality such as tantra (sex yoga) start with breath knowledge. There is no other ecstatic treatment. Your happiness card is Water.

Place a minute timer and sit down to take in the water in peace. Timers avoid us holding a clock to confuse ourselves. This gentle practice can feel like coming home to you, including giving yourself a tender love. Deepen the desire to let go of your brain and reconnect to the body during treatment by practicing a routine ocean relaxation method.

Ocean Breathing with a Partner
Five minutes to set the timer. Lean over against the wife or cross-legged her legs (with or without clothing on), or the female on her back. Watch the partner's left eye with a soft look. Be mindful of your eyes ' room. Remember your movement. Note your breathing. Is it fast, dense, natural, and uneven? Combine your changes slowly, holding your eyes soft.

Start to experience the sea together, both inhaling and exhaling your friend. Tell her to be more precise when her voice becomes inaudible. We were trained to move softly, so it could be a barrier for us to resolve to exercise in a more understandable way. Find a comfortable, steady tempo for you both. Love the permission to look at your loved one, sharing the same respiration and tone. Gently turn your mind to the wind as you run.

Be ready to tap differently. Often at some point, our brain is unable and wants control again. Just beyond this, a rich and tasty environment awaits trance. After a few minutes of breath observation you can assure the thinking mind that you will be back. You'll shortly expect to take a break from the usual ocean respiration awareness. It will be essential to practice the capacity of focus and awareness. The incentives will be useful if you are careful.

Finish the session of ocean breezing with a moist greeting. Place your hands together in the center of worship with your breastbone paws. Inhale the companion in detail, then turn to each other and exhale at the 3rd eye (also called the face of the brain, which is our source of intuition).

Create a Sexy Space

I was welcomed by my husband to a "Night of Sensual Ecstasy" year later to get an initial, creative invitation in the post. I had returned home after a few months, so he captured my attention. He gave me a bubble bath that particular night, read my poems, and served me raspberries lapped with cognac by mouth. Instead, he took me for an erotic massage into our house.

I couldn't remember our room to my shock. The bed was covered in fresh satin sheets and ample pillows. He'd restructured the walls with new pictures of ourselves–some nude–and other erotic art (all beautifully framed). The room had the feel and illumination of an ancient temple of candlelight and gentle music. The nightstand was lined with peacock feathers, bunny hair, tropical misters, oils, and lotions. Amazed, I stared at the sacred temple he built for us through watery eyes.

The internal shift of our lives was reflected in our transformed home. We dedicated ourselves to more fun. Our new sexy bedroom was a symbol of our further hot actions to lift our marriage's playfulness. I'd sit, think, and laugh as I went through the room during the day. Our passion was in the place.

Build your sexy room, be it a partner or not, in your home for your intimate meetings. Behavior is deliberate. Render your room special–let your dreams, history, legends, preferences, and desires to be an erotic shrine. Decorate it all at once, and distribute the work overtime, so let the room show you. Your sacred temple is a juggy spot of erotic massage discovery. You will smile, just passing by the door.

Body Caresses

The skin is the body's largest organ and becomes sensitive to touch when they age. Perhaps we can experience better because we can slow down and take the time to detect complexities of emotion. Contact awareness relaxes us into sexual transformation. Caresses transmit impulses directly to the sexual organs on the hands and feet. Touching these places produces a slight rise in sexual energy.

Cariousness of the skin is more sensual than physical. The fine brush is to experience the enjoyment of emotions at a period when lust is more directed at. Although physical interaction can be a natural result of sensual communication, this book teaches you a sensual touch or a joy to touch at the moment over a destination like sex. You will be excited about the trip instead of having to hit the gender target.

Take Turns

You will choose to be the active or passive partner for the exercises in this book and then change roles. You can slow down by taking turns to take notice of what's going on. When you are the active partner or touch giver, your fingertips or hands can focus on the sensations from touching the skin of your partner. You can be aware of every slight sense of touch if you're the active participant and recipient of contact. Alternating your action and your passiveness gives you the greater enjoyment because your time is new and hasty to experience the sensations.

Touch to Pleasure Yourself

For someone else's joy, they have learned to touch. We are programmed to look after the other individual in partnerships. It will seem different to feel your gratification, and this fresh style will design your caresses with energy and curiosity. You are in performance mode if you try to please your husband and therefore think about the work you do for him.

You're not in this present moment when you're thinking about "doing it wrong." You will allow yourself to relax and enjoy, and invite your partner to do the same when touching a partner for his benefit.

Preparing for a Caress

We always say, "Now I have my part, I will give back." In getting so much praise, we feel self-conscious and self-centered. Maybe we don't feel all this stuff we merit deep down. Turning will allow us to open up to more fun, to gain more. We know that we give him a precious gift by enjoying it entirely by being satisfied with the presence of our friend.

Consider the joy of petting a dog or a cat. Is it innocent of attracting so much publicity and cutting us off? Is it sitting up in the center of the hotbed because it's his turn? We appreciate them, and we understand how to welcome them, we milk with everything we are ready to give — shamelessly and unrelentingly — and we are satisfied like donors. Please allow your enjoyment to have a time limit. If you obtain (or offer, for that matter), be passionate, also sparkling.

Concentrate on Your Feelings

Position the hand of your companion, as you would a precious diamond when the giver is prepared. Only feel the heat between your feet. The warmth between your eyes. Since the hand's weight. The contour of the palm and fingertips starts very gradually. Close your eyes to discover each outline, crevasse, column, fold more effectively. Wonder about this hand that gave so much joy to you. Go and be amazed by your tactile exploration.

Cariousness is nonverbal, allowing the right mind to drive (it functions non-verbally, excels both physically, spatially, perceptively, and intuitively). Do not break away from this room with a tendency to talk or to react through movements.

A massage is not a caress. You do not control the muscle tissue below as you activate the nerves in the body. The smoother the contact is, often, the more relaxing. For one place, too much stress and stroking constantly destroys the emotions. Touch the skin just slightly. The foundations go down, and everything he's going to feel.

Try to touch steadily and more gently when you find it challenging to stay focused. When you lose concentration, stop feeling, take a break and, better yet, catch a pair of breaths with your friend. Silence is as powerful as a wave. When you pick up a friend with smoke, whisper in his ear gently that he is aware of the sea. The breath slows down your brain and allows you to stay focused, whether you send or receive. The key is a conscious movement.

Communicate with Compassion

You may want to caress the other hand if you feel that half the time frame has elapsed. This caress must start with the clock. Place your hand down gently, open your eyes, and caress with a welcome from your hands. Love how you have respected the eyes, cars, and work in the world through our imagination. Disable the clock and switch positions to ten minutes.

Chapter 3: Lubricants, Gels, Toys, and their Role

Lubes can sometimes be essential. The vagina can sometimes fail to self-lubricate enough for both of you to enjoy the intercourse session. Lubricants and gels are especially necessary whenever you are getting into anal penetration, simply because the ass is not capable of self-lubricating like the vagina.

In a nutshell, lubricants make sex more enjoyable and comfortable. The juices excreted by the vagina and saliva will not give sufficient lubrication to get the job done correctly. Even if you have some alone time and feel the mood to masturbate, whether it is with your hand or using tools, lubricants will help take your experience to a whole other level.

You need to have in mind that you cannot just use any lubricant or gel you find, you need to get one that is explicitly made for sexual intercourse. You can find a wide array of lubes in a majority of drug stores and in any sex shop you can find. Technology has made buying lubes even more convenient because you can order online from the comfort of your home and have it delivered to you; in some cases, delivery can be made within the hour!!

There are two main types of lubricants and gels that are available in the market, both of which come in various brands and scents, and we will have a look at them in this chapter.

Water-Based Lubricants and Gels

One quality of water-based lubricants that makes them the preferred choice of many is that they do not easily stain and cleaning them up is quite easy. They are also available in a wide array of tastes, textures, ingredients, and consistencies. These lubricants are also very much compatible with all the materials used to make sex toys, as well as those that are used to manufacture both latex and non-latex condoms.

You need to note, however, that the majority percentage of these water-based lubricants are manufactured using glycerine, and this can make some people uncomfortable or even cause problems. A large number of women attribute glycerine to be the cause of an imbalance in the yeast levels in their vagina and also yeast infections. This, however, does not affect anal sex, and therefore the preference for most people having the lube, which does not contain glycerine to avoid unnecessary problems. When it comes to anal sex, there are some people who find that lubricants that contain high levels of glycerine tend to stimulate their bowel movements, and prefer to avoid them when engaging in anal sex. No need to worry though, there is an increase in the number of lubricants that do not contain any glycerine, and also there are some that do not even contain paraben.

In terms of consistency, water-based lubricants completely cover that scale. They are available in varying levels of liquidity, ranging from super-thick, thick, medium, and also thin. Any lubricant can greatly facilitate penetration, but thick and super-thick lubricants are better suited for anal penetration. The reason is that they possess a consistency that is very similar to hair gel. They tend lasting longer and also protect the gentle rectal tissue by acting as a cushioning layer.

Depending on your preferences, if you always prefer yo put either your hands, sec toys, or even a penis in your mouth after they have come in contact with a lubricant or gel, you might want to purchase a lubricant that has a pleasant taste, or at least, a flavor that you can stand. Some water-based lubricants taste of chemicals or have a sour taste that is a significant turn-off. There are quite a number of sexual lubricants on the market that are flavored, and if you are not lucky enough to find your taste of choice in the first attempt, you may have to taste quite a number of flavors.

Among the current trends as far as water-based lubricants are concerned is warming lubricants. These lubricants create a warming effect upon contact. There are, however, various ingredients, and they are:

- Acacia honey or any of its derivatives (Astroglide warming liquid, wet warming lubricant, and KY warming liquid)

- Menthol (hot elbow grease, sliquid sizzle that is glycerine free, and ID sensation)

- Cinnamon back (emerita OH). It is the most natural among them all.

The honey or menthol generates a warming feeling that makes blood rush to the genitals, thereby assisting in the arousal process.

As far as lubricants are concerned, whether or not you like, it depends on your personal preferences and what you find comfortable. Some people believe that they love the way it causes their private parts to tingle; others have horror stories about them (probably did not know about the glycerine). A vast majority of women prefer warming lubricants because they have an element of protecting the vagina, but at the same time, many people find that they get an overwhelming feeling whenever they use this warming lubricants for anal penetration.

Silicon-Based Lubricants

Lubricants and gels that are made using silicon are quickly becoming popular among its users. Some brands that have silicone-based lubricants and gels include System JO Original, ID Velvet, Swiss Navy Silicon, Eros gel, Wet platinum, and KY Intrigue. Just like water-based gels and lubricants, silicon-based lubes are also do not stain. They, however, are odorless and are more expensive than water-based lubricants and gels because they do not dry up as fast (they last longer), and therefore you only use less lube.

Silicon gels are usually more concentrated and, therefore, can go a long way. A lot of people typically have a liking to silicon's slick texture and its fantastic quality of not being sticky or even tacky like their water-based counterparts. Some people claim that this sleek texture of silicon has a lot of friction, making it a better option for anal sex.

Silicon-based lubricants work well with both latex condoms and non-latex condoms and other safe sex barriers, a select number of materials used to make sex toys including glass, rubber, metal, and hard plastic. Sex toys that are made using silicon are entirely incompatible with silicon-based gels and lubricants as they get damaged. The only way that silicon sex toy lovers can get to lubricate them with silicon-based lubricants and gels is by wrapping them up with a condom. If you like to get a little freaky in the shower or a swimming pool, silicon-based lubes and gels are the best option because, unlike water-based lubricants, they remain slick underwater. This quality makes them the best choice of getting the job done in such scenarios.

Oil-Based Lubricants and Gels

Oil-based gels and lubricants and also those that are vegetable-based, whether you bought them or common household goods such as petroleum jelly, baby oil, or even lotions, are not recommended. The simple reason behind this is that they are very messy and leave behind nasty stains on whatever they come in contact with. They are also responsible for the breakage of latex condoms and the pieced sex dolls.

The most significant risk that these lubes have is that these lubes, and gels have a tendency of setting camp inside the vagina, and they cannot get flushed out of the body. This is very unhealthy to the woman because it becomes a perfect spot where bacteria can breed, and this will eventually result in a vaginal infection. Even if you use these lubes for anal sex, they always make their way to the vagina, and the result is the same. The best thing you can do to spice up your sex life is using oil and vegetable-based lubricants for their intended purpose, not sex. Men can, however, use them for masturbation, but make sure to rinse off your penis thoroughly before you can penetrate someone else.

How to Properly Use Lubricants and Gels

Using lubricants and gels is a pretty straight forward process. You need to apply it on whatever you need to insert, be it a penis, finger, or a sex toy, then slide it in. You need to remember that water-based lubricants and gels dry up quicker, and therefore you should use a lot of it and also be prepared to refill it halfway through. Silicon-based lubes do not dry up quickly, and therefore you can comfortably use it sparingly. You can have it around, though, to keep it spicy. A box of baby wipes or pocket tissues can also come in handy to wipe out any extra gel, spillages, or any other accidents that may occur.

When it comes to anal sex, sometimes it can become challenging to get the lube to where it is supposed to get. Luckily, two commodities are available in the market that can help solve this problem.

1. There is a soft plastic tube of the Astroglide Gel that has a long neck, and it is called the Astroglide Gel Shooter. What you need to do is to gently rip off the top and slip the neck inside the butt hole and squeeze the lube inside the anus.
2. Secondly, there is the Lube Shooter, and this is typically a non-reusable plastic syringe, and for safety, it has a flared base. There are two ways of refilling it:
    a. Take off the cap that is on the tip and place the tip in a bottle of lube. Pull up the plunger and draw the lube into it like a syringe.
    b. Pour your favorite lube into the barrel after removing the plunger. You need to know,

however, that this method can be a little messy.

Once it is full, lube the syringe tip and gently insert it into the ass. Push down the plunger so that the lube can be released into the ass. At your pleasure, you can refill the shooter and repeat the process.

Sex Toys

The vulva contains exterior lips, internal lips, scissors, frenuls, openings of the urethra, the clitoral hood, and the clitoral glans. The vulva comprises the outside labia. Many people describe the vagina throughout the entire genital area, but that is incorrect. The word Vulva and one I use in the entire novel is right. Outer lips are the internal lips of the vulva (also known as the labia majora). We have hair follicles and are, of course, rugged. You can brush, touch, kiss and even twitter them softly, and the internal labia are receptive. Within lips are the two hairless central lips of the vulva (also known as labia minora). It can be slim or small, wide and thin, one of them or somewhere between them. The inner lips are more sensitive than the external lips. They burst in color when a wife is turned on. It is important to know that the vulva of every person is different: some have big external lips, and some have small internal lips that are more prominent than their outer lips. Many lips of women are similar in size, some of the asymmetric. A sensitive area is a tissue where the internal lips touch on the bottom of the spoon. The skin with its inner lips at the top is the frenulum, and many females, especially as this position is near to the clitoral gland and cap, may be very responsive.

The hair that covers the clitoral glans, like a condom on a man's penis, is the clitoral cover. The clitoral glans are under the hat. This is the most responsive part of a woman's anatomy. The glass clitoral— many people simply refer to it as a clitoris. The nerve elements were 6,000 to 8,000. The clitoris is also a complex system of interrelated nerves, glands, muscles, and ligaments, not only in this tiny nude. The clitoris underneath the hood has a thread that runs down the frenulum from the glans. The clitoris legs are like two sides of a wishbone that extend all the way from the spine to the tip.

The urethral gap is underneath the clitoral glans between the internal eyes.

The urethra, about 11/2 to 2 inches long (3.75 to 5 cm) behind the pubic bone, carries the circulation. The opening of the uterus, the most sensitive part of the body and leads to the vaginal canal, lies behind the urethral gap.

Just inside the vaginal opening, you can touch the urethral sponge, commonly referred to as the G-spot, through the mask of the vaginal wall. Spongy erectile tissue, which includes glands and behaves, is the urethral sponge. Like the clitoris, the G-point is a network of nerves, muscles, and tissues, not just an isolated location for arousal. The drums in the urethral sponge filled with water when a person is turned on, allowing the sponges to swell.

This liquid is sometimes discharged into the urethra (or two conduits that are adjacent only to the urethra) through the paraurethral conduits. This is alluded to as vaginal and woman ejaculation.

The region between a vagina and the anus is the perineum that responds properly to massage and stimulation, a responsive, but sometimes ignored, erogic zone in the body.

The scrotal bag is the skin bag that encircles the testicles. The spring is the penis's main body. The prostate, also referred to as the head, is a man's penis ' most sensitive part because it has a nerve ending.

The hole where semen and ejaculate leave the body is the urethral gap.

The foreskin is extracted on a circumcised penis in order to make the head fully accessible. The crown, also known as the coronal edge, is the internal perimeter of the head that connects the head to the shaft. When you trace the corona line to the base of the cock, you will see where the two ends meet: This is the frenulum. Often the most vulnerable region of the head is this zone.

The unclear penis has a skin covering or securing the glans, and it has a foreskin. The internal pliers of the foreskin compose of mucous membrane which retains a clean, wet, and receptive glans ' layer. A high blood flow output and a heavy amount of nerve endings are found in the foreskin. The frenulum on an uncircumcised penis is the location of the foreskin on the bottom of the neck.

The perineum is the region from the base of the penis to the anal end.

Whenever you activate the perineum of a person, the tip of the penis, which runs within his skin, is activated.

The men and women in Anal Physiology have almost the same anorectal physiology, so this happens regardless of their sex. The anus is a soft tissue, abundant with nerve endings. The anus is the anal opening. It has a porous appearance and has hair follicles on the surrounding skin.

The outer and inner sphincter muscles were located inside the anus. These are the muscles that make the anus feel tight and regulate the bowel movements; they are the ones to be confident and comfortable anal penetration can be accomplished. The outside sphincter is closest to the door. The outer sphincter can be regulated, agitated, or relaxed. Think that you are carrying and expelling something in your butt. You strengthen the internal sphincter muscles when storing and relax and pushing down and releasing it.

On the other side, the inner sphincter is regulated by the autonomous nervous system, which also regulates unintended bodily functions such as the breathing rate. This muscle normally responds reflectively; for example, the inner sphincter is able to relax when you're ready to take a bowel movement, allowing the feces to travel from the rectum to and out of the anus. External and internal sphincter muscles may function independently, but they often operate together because they overlap. The more awareness and experience you have of the sphincters, the more toned and "in form," and the smoother and easy anal penetration they will be.

The anal canal, made of soft and responsive instruction with a strong nerve ending density, is the first inch inside the anus. The rectum, 8-9 mm (20-22,5 cm) wide, is beyond the anal duct; the rectum forms of loose, thin, smooth tissue folds. In contrast to the anal canal, the rectum will extend more than the anal canal if you are nervous, which enables penetration.

The rectum is not a duct but has two straight curves. The lower section of the rectum bends to the navel. The rectum stretches around to your backbone for a few centimeters and then down to your navel. Both the rectum and the colon curve side-by-side, and the two curve from person to person, whether they curve to right or wrong. Such curves are part of why the anal penetration, particularly at first, must be gradual and gentle. The rectum and curves of each individual are different, and it's better to feel your way carefully into the rectum after curves, instead of jamming something immediately through.

Anus, anal canal and rectum are all responsive and are therefore very pleasurable for anal stimulation and penetration. The anal canal's anus and external portion compose of the same delicate soft tissue, and this area comprises the largest nerve endings density in our anal anatomy. Overall, this tissue is more sensitive to movement and pressure.

The inner part of the anal channel and rectum comprise of mucous membranes with much lower ends, but the stress sensitivity of the tissue (for example, the penetration) is significantly higher.

The biggest gender difference is that people have a prostate organ when it comes to anorectal biology. The prostate gland is part of the man's urethra; it is behind a pubic bone, under the kidney, and above the base of the penis (sometimes called the P-spot or male G-spot). The prostate is around the size and shape of the walnut, a mass of bone, glands, and connective tissue; it produces ejaculation fluid, which combines the seminal vesicles with the semen and sperm to form male ejaculate. Inside an anus of a person in the front wall, the prostate gland is 1 to 2 inches (2,5 to 5 cm) so that it can be activated by direct anal penetration. Prostate stimulation can be very satisfying, and many people experience prostate stimulation orgasms alone or in tandem with genital stimulation. There is no prostate gland for females, but many still think pleasurable regarding anal sex.

For many men, the first sexual partner we have is ourselves, and masturbation is the way we get to understand our sexual selves. CHAPTER 2 SEX TOYS: The Way to Solo or Companion Pleasure While we move our skin, we explore new experiences, and seek various techniques. As we reach ourselves. A reward, an act of self-love, masturbation. Individuals masturbate with different intentions for a variety of reasons: pleasure, creativity, tension easing, sleeping (or waking up), or a connection to one's own skin. A doll is a great way to learn about your body and sexuality, improve your pelvic muscles, and relax them, change up your routine, and learn new things.

Their first orgasm, their first wet dream, and their first masturbation season are all practices for going through the culture. Many children tend to masturbate when they are at puberty. We discover how their cock functions and masturbate into ecstasy when they are young adults. Most girls have no parallel training, though. The first hard-on clitoral woman in pop culture isn't just a normal trend. Yet girls are not allowed in the same manner as people to accept their reproductive organs. As a consequence, most people either don't masturbate or never masturbate. This double norm affects females in their sexual development, and they often evolve with the impression of ambivalence, embarrassment, uncertainty, and humiliation on their own bodies.

A sex toy like a vibrator is a great way to introduce the concept for a girl who has never masturbated before. A vibrator can provide the support, error if she feels hesitant to contact her and uncertain about what to do.

In the same manner, a vibrator is often prescribed by sex therapists or doctors for people who have never had an orgasm or who have difficulty reaching orgasm.

Regardless of sex, you should not abandon self-discovery once you are sexually active. I have one bit of advice for everyone if people ask me for suggestions on how to become a better lover: masturbate. That's right: the more intimacy you get, the more you have to have sex with your partner. The secret to sexual health, well-being and happiness is self-knowledge. The more you learn about your own body— the more stuff you want, the more you can communicate with your friend, the greater you can be, who doesnâ t look, the more you can turn on, the more shut off yourself.

It's also a good way to try something different with a trick when you masturbate. You may want to experiment — with a vibrator, test a cock ring, and try anal penetration. Whatever it is, you may be intrigued, but you are unwilling to discuss it with your spouse or play with it. That's all wrong. That is all right. You must not automatically discuss with your spouse the sexual desire you have. Do it for a single session instead, then look at how you like it. You may choose to hold it to yourself and use it for your own enjoyment. Or you might consider it so much to you that you would like to share it with your friend.

It's not just enjoyable to perform physical fitness for better health, and it is really great for you! Just as we know that exercise is good for our bodies and leads to a reduction in the likelihood of certain illnesses and diseases, it is important to practice our sexual anatomy. Actually, a large part of male and female sexual wellbeing is the activity of pubococcygeal muscles (also known as the PC muscles). From the pubic bone the PC muscles go to the tailbone to protect the cervix, bubble, and intestine. Such muscles contract spontaneously for both men and women when you get sexually excited or rhythmically during orgasm. Men may enhance their prosthetic fitness, learn to control and postpone ejaculation, reduce incontinence, sustain stronger erections and have more flexibility during intercourse, through improving their pc muscles with workouts.

PC muscles for women can be strained, damaged, and atrophied by diabetes, pregnancy, and birth, during sexual abstinence, or as part of aging. You will better adapt to your emotions and sensitivity in your pelvic area by improving and strengthening your PC muscles. The movements often tunicate the pelvic muscles so that they are more relaxed and sensitive to enjoyable stimuli.

- Maintaining urinary tract safety
- Remove and regulate incontinence
- Preparation for pregnancy and birth
- Allow sexual tolerance stronger
- Improved satisfaction through clitoral stimulation, or vaginal and anal penetrants
- Get better-controlled orgasms Kegel exercises are approved to support the nurse.
- Maintains urinary tract health

- Avoid and manage incontinence.

You may do the exercises lie down, sit down, and rise, and during masturbation, the blood flow to your groin decreases, and the arousal rises. This should be done daily for best results, as is the case in other training regimes. Do not panic–this is natural if your muscles seem at first exhausted. The more you do the drills, the less toned the muscles of your PC are and the more practice you have. Use your common sense and do not overdo it at first; see a physician if you have any discomfort.

Dream to reach the PC muscles, you can stop peeing (or you can prevent leakage of urine when you are peeing). The PC muscles are the muscles you contract to stop the flow. In your uterus, you can also ride your thumb and begin pressing your hand into your muscles. Take a few deep breaths until you reach the PC muscles. Lock and keep the muscles for a few seconds. The muscles, instead of contract start adding a second to your practice and see if you can work up to 10 seconds of deal, then 10 seconds of rest. You can do it many times a day in groups of ten. Make sure you detach the PC muscle for best results.

Don't hold your breath and move your stomach or other muscles.

Many say that doing computer exercise workout with something in the uterus (or in the men's anus) produces better results because you operate the muscles against some pressure. Vaginal Exercise: Treat Ben-Wa Balls, Stone Eggs and Barbells Most items are specially designed for Kegel exercises.

Girls can be used to exercise their machine muscles with large egg-shaped toys made of polished jade, onyx, and other natural stones. You float into your uterus a well-lubricated shell, then practice locking up your muscles. Since it's both strong and dense, the muscles are more demanding. You can do the workouts sitting when the muscles are heavier. Ben-Wa balls are two spheres on a chain that is typically rubber or silicone. They're smaller and lighter than stones. To people bullied by the size and weight of the chickens, they are a good start. Balls should not be used for eggs or Ben-Wa anally.

Strong but not as heavy as sperm, physicians, sexologists, or Kegel practitioners are recommended to take vaginal barbells. The Kegelcisor or Betty's Vaginal Barbell are heavy metal dildos similar in design and have a span of about seven inches (18 cm). They weigh almost a pound and have balls of different sizes on both sides. You begin with clamping on the smaller ring, so you finish up while your muscle tone improves; many exercises call for muscle tension as you take the barbell out of your vagina. The natural contours Energie is a similar product except with a metal-coated plastic coating and a flat ball-free layer. The three can be used anally, however carefully, because they have no flared bases. Once the training is complete, barbells, Ben-Wa balls, and rock egg can be used for fun as sex toys as well.

The Vaginal Barbell Assisted Pleasure Balls Betty's Vaginal Barbell Assisted sex toys were designed to make fun and can support the sex life in multiple walks of life. While toys are long overdue since they have been known as marital supports, it retains one thing: they could solve problems.

Low libido, particularly when women get older, is one of the most common issues. A vibrator will help to end the party for women who have trouble getting excited. In males, erectile dysfunction is two of the most common problems with early ejaculation. Penis pumps can help you get an erection; a cock ring will help keep the erection healthy, prolong ejaculation and improve the marriage.

Women usually take longer than men to get excited. If the sex is not completely engorged because the uterus hasn't lubricated or grown before it is adequately warmed up the body is really not ready. The sex is not fully engorged. Many women who suffer discomfort during sex are clearly not given sufficient time to recover their bodies. To promote the waking phase, you can use all sorts of sex toys, including dildos and vibrators. You could make conceptual games simple and enjoyable, relax and mood you. Therefore, the penetration of a toy, which is slightly smaller than him is an excellent way to prepare if your companion is well prepared.

Sex toys will bring you an "extra set of hands" in your bathroom, enabling you to do two or three things at once! Imagine that you can concurrently bring her vaginal penetration, clitoral stimulation, and anal gratification. It can be assisted by a button tube, a vibrator or a dildo.

If you can not access other parts of your body by the perfect position for your contact, a vibrator may be there. What if you want to play concurrently with his cock, ass, and nipples? A tiny vibrator or nipple clamps will help you mask all of your hot spots.

Sex toys are a device to evolve: they extend the erotic range. One of the best things about sex toys is that it can help you stay away from a gender model all the time. Intercourse is often perceived to be the primary operation, the key thing to which you are operating. But the fact is that gender is not the only path. Many people prefer other enjoyment, such as teasing, manual stimulation, or oral sex. Many women can not orgasm through gender. There can be people who can't have sex. Women with high-risk pregnancy, birthright and certain states of age may not have sex as people with erectile or prostate dysfunction. Yet you can't have sex, and it doesn't say! Toys encourage couples to think outside the box.

Evidence has shown that many women require clitoral orgasm stimulation. A hand or a tongue is clearly not appropriate for some people. We need a strong, concentrated, and constant stimulus which people can not provide sometimes. Then, there are vibrators! Vibrators provide a different kind of incomparable stimulus. Many women find oral sex and manual stimulation amazing, turn it on, and get it on the top.

Just can't ecstasy it. You should hit the finish line with the vibrators.

Toys can be the catalyst to reinvigorate the sexual relationships for long-term partners. Sometimes it makes you bond with your mate if you bring something new and exciting into your sex life. Clearly, shopping for a new play item for many pairs can be a big turn-on.

You can say sexy things to each other while searching the shop racks, disclose what you want about a certain product and taunt each other with the openings. There is plenty more fun to come once you have made your order.

A guy I meet every Christmas orders his wife a special new gadget with a personalized card; it's now their tradition. He wants to find the perfect woman he purchases and shows what awaits her under the tree in excitement. For more than fifteen years, they had an enjoyable and fulfilling sex life.

The designs, swings, and sling of the liberator can leading to the change of the direction of penetration and aid and organizing the species in ways you never thought possible. Things like blindfold, oil relaxation candles, and G-spot devices could expand your sexual arsenal to new activities.

Toys also can set the stage for imaginary roles; sometimes, it takes a paddle crack to hold mean girls or boys in line! Eventually, there are explanations for sex toys: vibrators, dildos, and plugs: they're so much fun!

Top 10 Reasons for Adding Sex Toys to Your Sex Life

1. Try something new: in a long-term sexual relationship, it is possible to become frustrated and complacent. Take stuff up with a sex toy.
2. Go from good to great: Hot sex already? Work for you with technology and innovation to get it even warmer.
3. Have a fast: Sometimes you just have to get off soon. Why not render it escape and recovery shortcut?
4. See and say: take turns, each with a favorite toy, and masturbate for each other. You will be able to look at your companion and perhaps know one or two things from the results of your lover.
5. Stay up all night. Let's claim that your dick is through for the day, but you're not either.

Choose a game, and as many more rounds, as you want, you're free to go.

6. Take her over the corner: some people require good, constant clitoral stimulation, and only a vibrator will support them.

7. Achieve synchronicity: do you want to indulge in the same place at the same time? Concurrent feelings are necessary (and orgasms)!

8. Go to more: Whether you want to know how to get multiorgasmic, then, of course, toys help inspire him and her with different orgasms.

9. Double the pleasure: does your friend want to have fun once, nor do you not want to ask your neighbor to help? With a dildo or vibrator, you can be both positions at once.

10.   Build your own adventure: find sex toys as your favorite adventures in your romantic drama if your bedroom is your stage; be imaginative, enjoyable, and welcome your playful side!

Chapter 4: Orgasms

Since human sexuality has been medicalized, they have seen what defines an orgasm constrained by something like this: Body Part Time under Stimulus= Orgasm, which seems to be something like this. I have never been great in that sort of science, but I help consumers with orgasms combined. Mixed orgasms act like a "link the lines" match in which the points of our erogenous regions are. Blended orgasms historically could be a simultaneous combination of clitoral and vaginal sensations for women, at least. But what if a girl would come with a tickled clitoris and a licked elbow? Throughout my view, this is a mixed orgasm–this entails the erogenous zones of an adult throughout the body and the erotic reaction of' join the points.'

Position 1: Pretzel Sticks

Position 2: Change

Position 3: Switch And Scream

In "Getting Going," you've got to know where the specific erogenous zones (or note, over time they're going to change). You heard who the friend is in the first step. It chapter will allow you and your companion to see and to explore a variety of traditionally respected erogenous zones that motivate a lot of people, as well as a few places in and around your skin. The trick is to talk to your partner, which ones you toggle.

Getting Prepared

Because this chapter relies heavily on the body to reach and to enhance, cleanliness is essential. Think of taking a sensual bath or shower, with some dirty talk and suggestive words, to contribute to the workout. Therefore, a manicure or pedicure— professional or not — might be necessary, because the feet and hands are concerned.

To help you build different types of feelings — and every part of your body has an appropriate comfort zone — take out romantic scoundrels around your house and see what you can do. Maybe a linen, satin, or velvet item. A plum or something as light and suggestive when you're allergic. A tub of ice cubes and ice that you have preserved in different forms (popsicles are off-limits due to salt, which might contribute to a potential yeast infection).). You can also heat up in the water with stainless steel sets.

Massage oils with different natural essences could be available. Add a blindfold, any old collars for soft restraints, and brush over your partner's body to the list with your favorite music. Link with the erogenous zones of your mate and find various ways to encourage them. And if all of them don't know, inquire.

Warm-up

The above procedures were performed to guarantee identical care for both genders. He must satisfy the person before the first place and ensure that the guy is as hard as possible and able to enter her. She lays on her back, takes an item, and stirs it across her body to ensure that no erogenous regions are skipped. Maybe a feather over her pussy, a vagina ice cube, her mouth hands. Paint her erogenous areas of warm water in the bowl, or melting the candy, or a favorite jelly. Trace her back and between her thighs, wipe her clean with essential oils. When you have long sufficiently relaxed her side, she turns over and asks you to gaze at her front in the same way. She can, of course, be blindfolded to lift her other senses with her consent. It can be exciting to disable or suppress one of the senses, but it can also be terrifying so ask a question before you.

If you go outside the realm of vanilla, offer a safe word–a term you actually wouldn't use during your sex–which means stopping as soon as it is uttered. The evening events will seem all the more sexual once you have developed this level of trust.

If their erogenous zones are discussed and supported and when both sides agree that it is time to move on, they can change: from top to bottom, they will develop their back and front and try to incorporate as many concepts as possible. Investing in some love dices if you're failing and need suggestions about how to play and give your body satisfaction. You have countless ways to get the fireworks started as you turn for one part of the body and sexual activity on the other.

In the end, he is prepared for the next place, and the two of them ought to be wet from sweat, melting ice, and body fluids — the latter is the last target!

Tantalizing Hot wax

Hot wax is commonly applied to surfboards and hair removal aids, but consumers are also interested in testing something different before moving too far. Next, look for smell-less, colorless candles to thwart allergic reactions. The wax will then depend on how hard the candle is placed on the skin: the wax falling 6 inches (15 cm) down on its back would feel warmer than when dripped 6 foot (1.8 m), and the wax will not get any hotter. Drip any wax from different heights on top of your foot to measure the temperature. Eventually, remove parts of your body, like your ears and eyes, which you never would want to wax in. This can be a safe way for enjoying mild discomfort and intense enjoyment; always bear the pleasant aspect in mind. Play wax and flame cautiously and someone can get burnt.

Position 1: Pretzel Sticks

From a point, this may look like a woman on top, but some modifications gain its reputation and sexual properties in this role. The thrusts are quick and sincere, and at this stage you know what it means: the first quarter of her vagina is invoked. It also provides access for large legs, clitoral stimulation and a relaxed rhythm that both sides can reflect on everything that is happening.

Straddle him so that as long as you are on the bottom, he will reach you. Face forward as the foot land in his or her arms. Step forward. Push your shoulders and brace yourself on your forearms to encourage your entry if you want it to tongue you into your neck. Ask him where you want his hands to go. The back now is gone. The goal is to give the maximum possible amount of your erogenous areas.

Bring the ankles on them to make pretzel sticks curl. Use your arms, when your face joins in a loving hug, to gaze at your body in the direction of her. The goal here is to keep her legs tight — the key. If you have a mirror over you, the positive picture is that your legs should appear like a face, from your hips to your bottom.

Try to brush his feet, pause for a while, while you scratch and rub into him. The tension in your legs causes a contraction reaction that supports your pussy and cock. Suck your fingers and earrings to each other so long as you're fun. Make sure you talk to her for the "aural" gender.

Grind your body in and let it realize what you can do to make it more fun. Maybe if it flips his hands-on, you should keep it over his face, simulating light slavery. Rise and hang your breasts from the grasp of your lips. Then fire your guns and tell him to turn off your hands.

When she needs help with extra stimuli, put a hand or two, and when you turn over, she will do the same.

The process repeats to him above you, making sure your erogenous zones, such as your perineum–the gap between your rectum and your scrotum–are overlooked and provide the respect that they merit. Secure the legs around him, so that he can still sense the twisted pretzel's extra leg contact.

Give her the way she looked for it from you should she need to frottage (body-to-body rubbing).

There is no judgment, so if he wants here or there a thumb, a petal or an ice cube, give him the enjoyment he gives you.

Keep interacting with each other and let each other know when you are ready to move on to the next place.

This move trains you for the next position: a cowgirl side-saddle model.

Position 2: Move

In a push-up place, put your hands. Move down to your feet, behind his arms, so that he's not inside you anymore.

Sit on each side of him and move around him.

Place your knees on your back to spread your foot on the ground. This seems like you're ready to sit, but an arm extends to lie flat.

Sit down on his cock, kneel on his straight foot, and face the middle of his body to 45 to 90 °. You could put your hands everywhere, obviously, on the neck, knee, or ankle. If you don't need them for help, they are available to provide relaxation.

Position 3: Twisting and Screaming

The final position in this section should facilitate deeper penetration, thus providing an unmeasurable eye-to-eye and pleasing touch. Start to move your penis up and down. Use extra stimulation by grinding and naming one of the three or four feet. If you want additional stimulation.

Use your two hands-frees to meet additional requirements— to massage pecs or to touch their limbs or elsewhere. Use your hands to help her reach a pinnacle if your needs are met. You could switch sides. This might be true. The best way to stimulate your ass is to lend the hand away from you, and you can lease your hand too.

You can create a slight twisting move that may please you both with the small undulations of your hips. You can also switch this role from the other side, particularly if your penis bends to one side; you will be shocked by every difference.

Since kissing in this role is challenging, after kissing and sucking yourself, you should suck each other's fingers. It's like a long-distance hug for your friend!

There is no need at this stage to change positions, but to maximize stimulus. CRESCENDO You can regulate the deep and rapid penetration, and you can drive yourself into it if you have to mix thrusting with other sensations that you or your partner get from you.

Adjust the pace and intensity of your thrusts as you want further shaft relaxation. Make it happen, and ask for help with it if you need more turns— from touch, sound, scent, taste.

Speak of a combined orgasm as a linking activity. What does still needs to be connected? Could you, or do you have to ask for assistance?

Concentrate on yourself, your mother, and your two. Work to create an unforgettable experience without upsetting your mate. Tell how you can support her climax when you arrive first. Take a piece of the body and take a pet.

Take the two. Give a hand whatever it takes.

You can both be exhausted to reach and experience mixed orgasms.

Seek the moment and cuddle. Go for it if you want to start again.

Goodbye! All done! Well done!

Chord hitting can be as easy or difficult as the fusion of two or more of the erogenous zones in a dazzling sprint. Don't be trapped in the concept of "true" or "authentic" orgasm from somebody else.

Let the authorities disagree about what a "real" or "authentic" Stradivarius is, and call the mixed orgasms which you encounter. Oh, their "orgasms" from now on.

Chapter 5: Explore your Sexual Fantasies

Solo Fantasies

There is but one place to start: yourself. Whether you want to make your dreams genuine, invent a new fantasy scenario, make your masturbation better, and seek the peace of mind by knowing your fantasies. Fantasy emerges from within you, and how you like to use it.

Masturbation: Do it

All masturbaters, and although our emotions about it range from embarrassment to confidence and our masturbation sessions vary from robotic to joyful, we all share one aspect: we all believe in one thing.

Volumes of health benefits from masturbation have been published, refuting outdated misconceptions that have discouraged people from feeling better about this healthy activity. Masturbation is a relief opportunity for some individuals, something they would instead get around as quickly as possible.

Masturbation is known as something soothing, satisfying, and pleasant for others in all its ways. We do something positive to ourselves when we masturbate by taking nutrients and blood into our vagina and strengthening our pelvic muscles by holding them strong and healthy. Again, we get off, simple and straightforward–and it looks damn good.

Masturbation is where everything continues for us physically, from our first orgasms to our first experiences of how it influences us. This is the location for all our sexual experiences where we can return a sexual dictionary of our own unique words for comparison and knowledge. If we want to try something new, like tutorials for teenagers, vibrators, or an original sex method for a friend, masturbation is the most reliable tool to help get us off.

The imagination drives our sessions of masturbation. Even if our anticipation is solely physical, a warm fantasy may support a capable side. Combined pleasure, stimulation, and imagination can be an active learning tool:

- Faster, quicker, more efficient orgasm.
- Orgasm during acts of reproduction, such as oral sex, anal sex, or the sexual relationship.

- Overcome sexual apprehension and discomfort, such as intimacy with a new partner, tension anticipation, nervousness of trying new things.

Adjust sexual habits; for instance, try to masturbate new sensations such as anal sex or mild discomfort (S / M), increase or decrease in intensity.

Fun Masturbation Sessions: Fantasies, Sex Toys, and More

You have your dream, so you love focusing on it — how can you make it more accurate? Comfortable: a little predictive, and perhaps a shopping journey or two.

Public Masturbation

Community visions about masturbation are challenging, but not unthinkable. Know the civil sex laws in your community very well. If you're arrested, you probably won't be as hot in real-world as in fiction — or at least charged and arraigned. Make sure nobody's going to see you. It's part of the thrill and the danger; however, you engage him or her in a sexual act without his or her permission if someone recognizes you, it's not all right. Check predictably remote areas such as a secluded lake, a desolate natural environment such as a beach or woodland, an empty storage area, a vacant movie theatre.

Many spots in big urban centers are considered to be community spaces —use them if you're a resident and know the area. When you have to drive, take caution on the street. Rooftops might seem public and yet privately owned. Think away before you are aroused. Check around first. Think of places to hide, ways to disguise your company, or an authority figure telling a story beforehand. Keep it as warm and enjoyable as you can–an exciting encounter that can never be precisely duplicated with public masturbation.

You can add your dreams in living color to your living room with unobstructed views. The actions that render you sexy can exactly be shown by pornographic videos and images in porn books and magazines. You could physically fall into the scene as you masturbate into orgasm. The girl in her mouth "becomes" the male penis; the man who penetrates it "become."

Explicit Images

Mirrors bring pornographic images at the next point for someone who is already in contact with graphic sex and who never has seen himself near and sexually stimulated can be excellent learning. To make the dream more vivid, you don't want porn–some might even consider it distracting and disagree with the format. Nonetheless, the best picture will always be in your heart! You may provide your sights with a well-placed mirror, by gazing at your whole body and genitals while you masturbate. You may have a little mirror in your room or on the ground and sit in front of a large mirror to play in different positions. It's twice as hot when you see every step your hand makes to drizzle and rub on yourself –and don't be afraid to speak filthily.

Sex toys are not only great tools to masturbate–but they also create great ingredients for your creative situations. Gender fantasies— anal sex, oral sex or masturbation, S / M — can be replicated using several sex toys and appliances. Would a dildo render this team sex dream possible in your mouth? Would a device boost the scientific imagination? Take the dungeon to life with a nipple clamp?

Here are a few tasty unclean items and ideas: dildos are non-vibrating phallic sex toys used for stimulation and can be used in a wide variety of fantasy scenarios. Everyone "required" to suck his dick could roll the dildo across his face and drive it into their mouth again and again, and with one hand that you do as you masturbate with the other. Every fellatio dream can be enhanced by the dildo, and considering team sex with multiple dildos is even more enjoyable. If you put a dildo in a belt, gender gaming takes off while masturbating the dildo and you. The concert will be boosted by vibrating dildos. Masturbation in Dildo, combined with fantasy, is an excellent way of learning from penetration how to orgasm.

What to Stick in Your Ass

Even if at the moment you've got no anal toys? You have undoubtedly heard urban legends about people going to the ER with all sorts of strange or potentially lethal things in their rectum— and sadly, many of them do. Don't take hasty anal play toys to call.

Take the right judgment while rubbing your ass: they speak about preventing humiliation or extreme inequality, even if you are shamed and unwilling to admit what excites you. Always use a lot of lubrication, but if the skin is well-lubricated, it sheds around the anus. Do not place in your pocket — or anywhere in your pockets— which has sharp edges, can crack, move, smash, or have a solid basis for functional recovery. If you can not pull it back securely, you can continue to act in your urban legend. Your anal pulling sphincter takes everything inside. Carrots are wrong– get the right tool for your work, like a butt plug or a discreet dildo for anal usage.

Anal devices make anal sex dreams more sensational. Others may like to pleasure themselves from their own hands or the "risk" of a thumb or a little plug to inject anything into the anal sex scenario. Anal beads, gradually and quickly based on their desires, can be added one at a time, left in or taken out. Alternatively, you can pass on, become a dream "anal princess," and use bigger butt plugs to relax while contemplating a group of anal slaves who will support you with a love sling.

Larger devices, properly used, can make you feel more "violated," and any manipulating tool may be used to strengthen the illusion of power taking, or "using." Butt plugs can be placed or left in place during another operation, to several fantasies, such as the possession or bondage of the skin.

Masturbation sleeves bring to the normal one-or two-handed movement a whole new level of feeling. Such sizes, thicknesses, textures, and shades come in a variety of forms –pick the one you consider most appealing. Some might find some of those toys crapy with the little plastic buttholes, while others might think it erotically fascinating. Would that raise the imagination with a porn star for having anal sex? Check it out. If titfucking is your dream of the day, your next session might be influenced by semi-real shaped breasts. Such things were inoffensive, though. Having them doesn't mean that you have sex with a part of the body or that you can somehow have sex with the whole person. Explore and fully enjoy your fantasies— at least, when you masturbate your cock, you'll experience a new feeling.

Sensation and S / M games are much more relevant to your pleasure/pain desires. Please be careful when playing alone with discomfort, servility, fire, asphyxiation, or any game that causes strong feelings. Brief clamps and clips can easily be added to improve pinnacle emotions, but note that when you pull them off, they hurt a lot more because the blood rushes back to the already clamped region. Such articles can be purchased in a sex toy or S / M department, hardware shop, or paper shop. Check them before you shop with the soft flesh of your leg–it can be deceiving, and it can sting worse than it seems. Make sure the videos are lined with rubber and do not buy your clips with teeth.

Fleshy parts of your body can include clicks and clamps: breasts, boobs, stomachs, legs, hips, penile skin and testicles, and lips and lumps! Place the videos in line with your fantasy situation, but don't place them on longer than your masturbation.

Such S / M situations are hard to replicate and to damage. When you may float, it isn't at all advised to bind yourself (handcuffs, ties, restraints, silk scarves, etc.) Asphyxiation is very dangerous to try, although it is not rare as a fantasy, and can be deadly all too often. The electric play leaves plenty of room for error — lethal mistake — and should be made solely by electricity professionals and studied by an S / M professional. Blindfolds are all right as long as you can't see comfortably.

Change Your Habits and Teach yourself new Skills
When you look at a picture, see a cinema, read a story, or get an idea, like in damp bunnies and stiffening cock, you get an image that fits for you. You know how to change the way of life and thinking. You do. You will know how to exploit your orgasm fantasies. Take a moment to remember the last session of your masturbation. How great did you feel?

What were you thinking? What were you thinking? Have you had a picture in your head in mind? Did you watch a video of cold porn? Don't think about it being "healthy," "evil," or suitable— you're using your sexual imagination only now as a device. Think of how it began, how it developed, and what prompted you to come. You probably started with an idea; somewhere, the photos or the activity intensified and then came to a climax coinciding with orgasm. Consider the end of your orgasm, the beginning, and the update–that's how you turn on.

Digging through what you have recently become is a tactic to get revived again, and to relive the past provides a leap to better control and intensification of your anticipation. Switch on, or try something new — be as happy as possible to stand up and see what images show when you're near to orgasm.

Take your time masturbating and continue as slowly as possible to boost, enhance, consistency, and experience numerous orgasms— guys, orgasms without ejaculation, for instance. Seek to go up to the height of anticipation, but you should not allow yourself over the edge — longer than you can, the unavoidable. Tantra practices utilize deliberate respiration and gradual sex methods to achieve powerful orgasms. People can learn to hit the orgasm's edge and, using the "squeeze" method, return and eventually grow to have several orgasms, i.e., come without ejaculation.

The squeeze is an easy way to avoid getting ready before you or your girlfriend (and you don't have to use the potentially damaging — and questionably effective—"delay "creams or sprays). A method for men: Squeeze strategies This squeezing takes place with the fingers positioned on the coronal surface, on the edge of the penis so that the thumb is on the underside of the penis and frenulum. Stop all, mostly hallucinations, and squeeze for three or four seconds when you come close. Many people think it works better to pinch at the base, and others find it works just like pushing their balls down away from the body– playing with how you respond. For more details on men's orgasmic strategies, please take Mantak Chia and Douglas Abrams from The Multi-Orgasmic Guy.

You will learn new erotic techniques— and love them much— using your newly found ability to conjure your dreams. The orgasm is probable when using pleasure, stimulation, or imagination methods while paired intercourse or something from which you usually don't climax, such as oral or anal sex. It is a step by step, but the commitment is worthwhile.

If a new technique, such as deep throat and vaginal fisting, is to be introduced into your sex life, continue fantasizing as you masturbate. Know how much about the new activity, whether you feel nervous or scared.

A Women's Tool: The vibrator women who use vibrators regularly to masturbate take their comfortable buddy on their dream explorations or girls who never experienced an experience could also give him a clue. Vibrators — or massagers — are perfect ways to express that enthusiasm. Some female vibrators would give them quick, thrilling, and consistent orgasms, even if they had difficulty reaching orgasm. Choose a vibrator that looks good to you, and schedule a time to take advantage of your new toy without disruptions or interruptions. Start by vibrating your inner thighs and gradually get to your genitals. Speed and stress test add the vibrator to your solo dream experiences-and double the enjoyment after a few pleasant play sessions!

Fantasy is the most powerful way to overcome masturbation problems, utilizing methods like above. Think, for example, when you masturbate on your abdomen, you usually cum silently— but you want to know clearly as you stretch your legs on your back. Or you want to climax with penetration, perhaps switch a fascination with certain clothes, such as masturbation. The shoes still keep you on, but you can also know how to appreciate certain sexual activities, change them up, and make your sexual life more enjoyable.

Start by getting excited in the manner you most understand and use your reliable methods of masturbation to bring you to the edge of orgasm. At this point, find the facets of new behavior that you are most interested in — if it's anal sex, is it the original idea of anal stimulation, or is it "dirty?" Make sure you masturbate and fantasize about the new activity so that you can climax yourself with the warm fantasy— the evaluation of the new behavior — when you arrive. Repeat until the experimenting is ready for the next level, which could require many sessions of masturbation.

- Get on before trying anal penetration, Four laws for masturbation
- Start gradually. Move steadily. So, so late. Very, very slowly.
- Tons of lube is used.

- Next, taunt yourself with relaxation and internal stimulation. Penetrate masturbating.
- In your butt, don't bring something dangerous.
- Slow down, apply the lube, and adjust the tasks if it hurts.

When you feel fascinated, pair your imagination experiment with sex toys that can mimic pleasure, like an anal insert or a fellatio dildo, and watch porn graphically portraying the fantastic sex you want to seek.

Toys will allow you to understand the anal feeling and to establish the link between pain and comfort. The use of dolls in masturbation helps your body to enjoy the sensation while you are adequately controlled. Play with flat, unbreakable items that do not have a foundation, so they can not slide and stick fingertips, and plenty of lubricant depending on the heat. The anal tissue is soft, so there should be anything broken or rough.

You will slowly become more comfortable— and enabled — by attempting your dream in real life, and this may push you towards some steamy meetings.

If you want to learn to thrust a penis profoundly by using imagination or stimulation, do it as often as you need with a dildo before you get it in a real, live person. Get a dildo with a flaring end so you can easily stick on it— nothing you can do to detach from your grip or throat (no bananas or cucumbers). Breathe in the dildo and maneuver with the rotating reaction while you hold to your orgasm and your hotter desires (preferably fantasies like fellatio). Unlike anal sex, deep-throating takes patience and exercises.

You can use the above techniques to make your excitement fit in with your partner to teach yourself orgasm during sexual intercourse with someone else or while you give or receive oral sex. You need not fantasize about what you do while you do it–this lets you get the sense of what you do, but likely this isn't your new dream number one. What will get you revived and head straight into ecstasy is what keeps you on, so picture what makes you cold? Use your creativity, which fits for you and your lover's pleasure to come.

Many may find the idea of fantasizing during marriage rather disturbing. It's easy to feel that you're uncomfortable if you have sex with your sweetie, and your mind is somewhere else — though you're not, at the very least. You are right there with them, they inspire you, and you satisfy your part of the deal by functioning seamlessly in the way you do best to express your joy with them. You don't do anything wrong; personally, when you have an orgasm, you do what everyone else has to do–you use imagination to improve the anticipation, enhance the pleasure and bring variety to your sexual life. A vision is nothing more than something that happens for you, whether it's a recollection or a concept, and you can fantasize about your present relationship while doing sexual activity.

Fantasies for Couples

Our indulgence is something we are committed to and able to share with others. Seduction. Seduction. Mastery. Amazingly. An apparatus, atmosphere, or guidance that renders you attractive and inspires passion. Each shift is exciting to watch your wife. Become a sex toy of his or her own. Taste something different that you wanted to try always — with spectacular success. We are prepared for a beautifully hedonistic, romantic feast as we gorge on one another the tempting treats of sexual fantasy.

You can be swept from Kansas to Oz when you and you enjoy uncorking a magic bottle that holds your sexual fantasies. Sexual facts could render your usually great sex life spectacular, from an imagination flushed over during the lovemaking to a costumed role-playing game. Phantasies not only sizzle your mutual sex life, but they also bring your confidentiality to the next stage, expand communication lines, and enhance your senses. Fantasies are packed of suspense, excitement, risk, happiness, and love. And you can post them beautifully.

Are you constructing a Fantasy scenario If you imagine a particularly hot sexual position, maybe a twist or two, like making it public or seeing beautiful strangers? Do you become activated? Even if the elegance of dreams focused on imagined experiences does not reveal their potential of suspense — no makeup or different colors of lifestyle.

Fantasy simulations may take the idea "secret handwork" and provide it with a context— such as a theatre for films, a bar, an office, or a ride. Take the imagination and the fake handwork at the movie theater is from the alien seated next to you; it is from a waiter in the diner, and it's from someone at the workplace who wants the job you recruit. And you're turned into role-playing quickly if you attach costumes and props, clearly defined tasks, a plot with a start, the halfway point, and a conclusion.

Specific dream possibilities come in infinite variations. I suggest that you use your imagination and anticipation as a barometer to decide what will work best for you— you don't use your intellect. Combine fantasy elements that both trigger and tend to combine: a sex act, a piece of clothing, a location, a difficulty.

You and your friend were able to participate fairly— e.g., 69 behind a truck. Or you might call one-shots, run the show, enjoy the ride with the other one (or be "required" to join).

Here are some tips for launching you. You may draw up your imagination list of things that are cold and unsettling. You or your partner can select "yes," "no" or "maybe" next to each object to get a clear idea of what you would want to be playing with or to copy the lists below.

Sex Activities Masturbation of the penis, the mouth ejaculation, female ejaculation, genital penetration, pants, threesomes, two men, many spouses, sex toys, male receptive anal penetration, female receptive anal penetration, different roles, for example, doggie, being a core of the sex

None(nude), hangers, lingerie, men's clothes, neckties, briefs jumper, pants, boots, shoes, socks, fabric, elastic, latex, cotton, bandages, neck, wedges, linen, clothesline, frames, ribbons, bows in head, pigtails, bottles, skirts, formal dresses, tiaras, looking things including wedding coats, slippers, baths

Places and predictions Household (kitchens, offices, closets for the furniture, showers and toilets), vehicles, workshop, bike, fireplaces, barns, woodsheds, lake, pubs, aisles, dungeon, sex party and poolside, watching porn, especially sex act) Places and pillows, beaches, restaurants, bars (in a park)

Have you ever seen anything on these lists? A recollection spark? Well known sound? You may pick what things you want to render possible in the realm of imagination and work better. Most partners are more involved in playing with threesomes by imagining that there is a third partner in bed (with your most motivated dirty talk in fantasy) than by trying to find a right third partner. So bringing your husband to an imagined dog house in your bathroom is much better than chaining him back into your courtyard. In endless variations, you could mix imagined and specific circumstances, characters, and objects to optimize fantasy scenarios that enable you.

Face, or in reality?

How "true" it is to you to create your dream. When it comes to fantasy playing in your marriage, you have many choices. You can: • Hold your thoughts to yourself, enjoy them while coupling, and enjoy them for masturbation.

- Share your ideas and scenes during intercourse with one another by talking.
- Admit a dream you want to try— this may spark hot sex— even if the fantasy stays in the discussion.
- Talk about your ideas freely together and think about how you want to make them more practical.
- Build the situation in which the imaginations are realized.

Successful fantasy games need to take careful account of the situation, the pacing, and the physical and emotional comfort. This needs common sense, particularly. Facing it, the idea of playing a female employee who has been captured by a fantastic police officer— and hauled in handcuffed for a glamorous afternoon at the jail— might sound attractive, but it isn't enjoyable for anyone to get arrested.

For every fantasy that you make, from the fun wearing of slippers under a commercial suit to the duty of your boyfriend to have sex with a biker gang in a gas station. Accept both comfort and security criteria and mutually determine how far you want to push the creativity. The treats under his clothes may be sweet, but he might jeopardize his urinal behavior— or make his stall all day and feel uncomfortable rather than attractive. Or it could be part of your dream to feel uncomfortable: a quiet embarrassment that you don't have to provide for yourself. You won't have to worry — but you won't know how far in the creative mind, and what the boundaries will be to ruin the fun. You won't feel embarrassment. Likewise, the notion of "driving" your wife into sex can satisfy, but it can respond quite adversely to being bound, pulled around, or taken by surprise. On the other side, he can sincerely crave all this and worry that you don't go far enough.

A famous pornographic author, one of my closest friends, shocked me when I said to her about this novel. I had a confession. She was thrilled to hear that people want to live out their dream have a tool and needed it to be around for her when she offered almost anything almost a decade ago to have her husband spank her. "I had to be spanished still. But it took me two years to raise and tell my courage — and he was murdered! Another year I lived with him, and I felt depressed. She was too angry when I confronted my first husband because she thought it was' degrading' to girls, and he would never do so in the millions of years, and when she decided to be spanked, I assured him that it was the reverse. He went to my house about a week ago and purchased a hard backed comb, although he was always reluctant to take it, although I feel that's most of the time because he didn't know why. You may have the courage to ask for what you want, but it doesn't mean that you are fulfilled with excitement, or that, if you are, your partner has the knowledge and the ability to perform your wishes as you want. Opening up can be terrifying, and even more disturbing is being greeted with fear, disappointment, and disgust. You will want to start learning how to communicate with each other and seek suggestions for starting the conversation.

Whether this is a lighthearted sex game or the unveiling of your most dark erotic dreams, imagination communication will bring you closer. You will figure out the most erotic secret desires of each other. Like excited teenagers on their first day, you are on a sexual adventure that takes you far away from your old sexual routines.

Your willingness to try (or at least discuss) new things gives rise to optimism. This is perfect for the friendship you have with each other. Our imaginations emerge from our deepest parts. We welcome someone else into our most private world once we reveal them. Emotionally exposed, it's simple. You have to trust your partner to refrain from assessing your skill, quality, and even more scarce imagination.

While such concerns can primarily be discussed by their talks, it becomes possible to increase confidence and to maintain this optimism over time. Not all will feel vulnerable to posting or dream screening. Some are empowered; many feel free to express themselves emotionally at last, and many more love the oral pleasure of speaking out loud about their wretched fantasies. If you let your desires go crazy, it can not just make your sexual relationship intense, vibrant, and alive.

Most people find affection incredibly hot. Couples in long-term ties also find that incorporating dreams and role-plays to their physical practice opens up a whole new realm of sexual satisfaction, creates deep connections, and returns their vitality into the good old days of socialization and trial. You could set off some pretty powerful sexual chimes if you and your partner experiment through illusions as you would with a new sex toy.

Know your Lover's Fantasies

Getting to know your lover's imaginations It is as easy — and maybe like wrecking your lover's motors— to figure out what gets your lover going. You will want to read the whole chapter before you go to search for sexual gold when you frequently speak about gender, but sex is not a standard subject for you. Tell your friend what their dreams are, talk to them about some of your expectations, and see at the sparks fly. Or you can mention and share five sexual fantasies you are involved in. If you're a little tentative, but you can say that you're ready for something new, try to find out what they're involved in — a film scene of them catching a breath, a stuffy erotic novel on the nightstand — and ask them in a provocative manner what they like.

You will start to prepare your scene once you have a fantasy subject in mind. First of all, decide what the creativity is and to whom it refers. Is it your fantasy, your partner, or both? Is it your creativity? You already have all the dream elements in your mind if it is yours, and you have only to give details to your friend. See the first section of your fantasy thoughts if your concepts are too sketchy to put into words— I advise you to read them together. Choose a sex activity, a costume, a pose like dominate and submissive or tell your partner what the dream is. Once you know who needs to do what, determine how particular this situation is. You can remain in the realm of imagination, view scenes in adult films, and read each other's romantic stories, which represent your fantasies. In this way, the mind is a vicarious thrill, unbelievably hot and perfect for anxious couples. This is a great experience. You also get the pleasure from your sweetheart dream, or the comfort of seeing your face seeing (or reading) your number one switch.

You may go further with your fantasies and take a hot talk to sex, where the behavior of imagination in depth is represented by one participant. When you go about your daily sexual practice, you're getting contextual narrative.

You don't have to talk like a diva, a sexy porn star, to reflect your sex fantasies. Remember that the meaning of your vocabulary will be the subject of your lustful audience, not your language inflection or voice quality. Enable yourself to fall into the tale and feel free to fill in the air; it's a motor mouth that is for you.

Do you not know what to say? What to say? Accurately describe in as much detail as possible what you do or what your friend does. Let your definitions of sex bloom into a scenario you know you're going to like. For, e.g., when you sat on his face and strove his cock at the same time, describe the scene as if two of you were doing these things to him. That's — threesome dream moment!

Sexy surprises Quick seductions and mutually crafted dreams are among the most exquisite pleasures of life; however, they shock you with something you feel they would like for you to do. Be sure your partner understands something is imminent. Take care that you are not tired, have a rough day, or want to shave before you see. Prepare for a pleasant surprise ahead. Buy, get buttons, wear the right gear.

Surprise your friend for a sweet sexual surprise like an aphrodisiac or full-body erotic massage or read a fun tale (possibly one with your favorite).

- Stick a note telling them what they'd like to do together. So do it. So do it.
- Let your bags in your pockets, send them a letter with directions, leave an erotic image where they locate them, or bookmark an erotic novel, which you'd like them to learn.
- Stun you and execute one of your dream sex acts (like anal sex).
- Once you come home with a beautiful dress, welcome your companion once you realize that they like it and plan it for you to be turned into.
- You may be in a suit, a schoolgirl costume, wash in the bathroom, "take" the shower (or watch porn, read a filthy novel, or what you shouldn't be doing).
- Transform your features in a sexy way, use romantic panties, and shaving your genitals. Try

going out and tell your partner at dinner on a date that does not wear underwear.

The Sexual Buffet Decline takes many forms, but it may be the most thrilling and sensual dining encounters to give your lover a taste. Drizzle onto any part of the body that asks to be licked cocoa syrup, honey, and strawberry sipped and slathered creams. Nibble on the fruit you put on your skin, slip a delicious bug over your genitals and consume it in full view. Place your partner's meal on the boiling, excited torso (especially finger food such as sushi) and eat your sweet fill.

Make sure that your vagina does not contain sweets and that your diet is not analyzed (ever).

When you talk to your friend, Erotic thoughts will grow as quickly as you want to create a shared fantasy— as long as you wish. You could press emotionally, or share a lot of the same desires with your friend. And what you want, you must ask. A mixed response may be given — part interest, part terror. Some people are reluctant to even think about dreams, and some may be refused.

In any scenario, one of you wants to come up with an idea together — easy if you frequently chat about gender in your marriage, overwhelming when you never. In any case, it can seem daunting to tell your partner that you want to try something new— and if the dream makes you uncomfortable, this is an underestimation. Yes, it is sometimes also difficult to think about talking about sex!

If you have something that is known and tested about gender that you think can make your partner feel insecure, too, ask him or her that you want something to improve. This is particularly true of your sexual fantasy before you encountered your current partner. It requires quite a lot of grit to speak up and ask for something you want, but also to know more about what your partner enjoys or dislikes. And you can get what you want!

Until you do something, put yourself in the shoes of your partner: If you're still typically not talking about sex and then one of you needs to, it could start to get angry. If you had personal secrets all along, your partner would wonder. Your discovery of this romantic treasure trove will most definitely also give your partner the chance to tell you about sex.

Consider how you can make the subject feel safe for yourself: do you feel like watching a film that looks like your dream and reflecting on it after the show? Or do you think that you would be more comfortable waiting for your companion to get romantic and then tell you what they think of fantasy trading? You can also try to say that you want to reveal a fantasy—sex — and not have to respond instantly. Ask them that you can resolve things later; it allows you all the time to let the thought settle down.

Find ways to encourage your friend to listen to you. Tell them to suspend judgment before you realize how much fun you expect both of you will have — and how necessary their presence is for you. Make sure you tell him or her to be incredibly sexy and not to speak until you feel confident that you can share your deepest wishes. The partner has to know that they are the show's highlight–and that you can get stronger than you ever were. The main thing to consider in preparation is how you can help your partner feel comfortable. Mentally rehearse, once you have a discussion, what you want to convey. Talk about how your companion will respond, so you are prepared to take whatever direction the argument can go.

The partner may not want the erotic dream to be checked for a variety of reasons. Or you may wish to your companion to make you happy, but don't know what to do. The knowledge of these issues will help to talk constructively about the uncertainty of your friend, how to resolve doubts that can prevent one of you, and what to do if one person feels all right about the other.

It may create powerful feelings if your partner desires to physically attempt something that you are fearful of, unclear, or spiritual. The application of any new sexual activity to a marriage can sound like a case of making or breaking, and sometimes it is. Asking you to try forms of sexual intimacy can render your interaction more successful or can pose so many issues that the ship rolls — a little too much often. Fantasy will reach you at the heart if someone feels unsafe, unaware of the intentions of his companion, and deeply uncomfortable. This is particularly true in the case of deprivation, anxiety, gender, age, and violent fantasies.

You may be concerned that somewhere inside a wrong person, a person who "deserves" something harmful— or worse, you would like your dream to be real if your sexual fantasy simultaneously causes you uncomfortable and ridicule you (or, confusingly, excites you) at the moment. Fantasies of rape and incest are not rare but extremely disturbing. Such dreams are just that–illusions–and thus, they live in the realm of imagination or the security of fiction interacting with anyone you know.

Only imagination implies you don't want to see it put into effect.

Up to play? Are you armed for play?

You are suitable at playing now! Fantasies of natural sex acts can be performed when you're always prepared and wherever you want, with specific scenarios. Make sure you have protection. Home is the perfect place to play your game, so virtual sex partners will meet you with a little fancy talk and creativity to change the time and position you want, and you are free to use sex toys, fetish, and accessories to add to your enjoyment.

Take the time when both of you can be irritated and rest, turn off your mobile, make sure your roommates are genuinely home and give the children to a sitter. Make sure you search for products and items like a dog collar, whipped charcoal, full-length mirror, massage oil. Have your papers prepared beforehand or, if you are heading to the house of your wife, take your therapies. (Don't neglect your unholy imagination!). Above all, give a sense of sexual adventure and comedy as vision is just that — play.

Chapter 6: Sexual Health

Our main principles of healthy male sexuality are shared with you.

These are accurate scientifically and important to you personally — the role of having a strong sexual relationship that is satisfying. We will explore how you can organize your thought (knowledge), understand your feelings (emotions), and control your actions (comportations) wisely. The ten issues that men should remember for sexual health in table 2.1 are discussed.

Table 2.1: The 10 Things Men Need to Learn for Individual Sexual Health

1. Make sure that sexuality is a part of your personality.
2. Appreciate the relational aspect of sexuality and not view it as autonomous.
3. Let your expectations regarding your bodily needs be positive and genuine.
4. Treasure the five functions of sex in your life (table 2.2).
5. Understand that it is better to settle for sex that is good enough rather than a mediocre one. It is more

true, gratifying, and of high quality.

6. Be an intimate team with your sexual partner and value them as a sexual friend.

7. You need to be smart in how you express and regulate your sexuality.

8. Appreciate the liking and worth of the sensation of touch.

9. Make sure that your real-life and your sex life are intertwined.

10.   Be cautious of the three methods of sexual arousal and integrate them into your sex styles as a couple.

These are the positions that help to make you a sexually healthy person and to make sexually healthy relationships easier for you.

Such features include the multiple goals of sex, the three types of sexual excitement and how to use them, the importance of managing the sex drive safely, and the importance of having sex as a collective romantic group.

It can be quite difficult to accept and incorporate into their lives for most people. Each theory will be discussed in-depth and asked to take part in a training session and read an example. First of all, though, we

ask you to come across a group of five or six men—
whether a sports team, working group, neighbors or
old friends. What do you think would happen if you
spoke to them about whether it was what they should
know and learn? Be real, not wrong in politics. If you
don't have a genuine, diligent group of friends, it's fun,
humiliation, jabbing, fun and diverting from the real
debate.

What if spouses and wives were part of this group? We
bet that the women will play a large part in the debate
and win it, personally. It would most likely turn into a
negative dialogue about why men can not open up in a
relationship and be honest about their feelings and
gender. The book does not deal with marital issues.
They encourage men to be conscious of and proud of
their manhood and sexuality.

There are too many male basses, and we have to fight
them. To man, women, sexuality, and relationships, it
is harmful. We promote principles that allow you as a
person to have faith in gender.

Healthy sex is an integral and optimistic aspect of
manhood. Sex can serve many beneficial roles in your
life, including enjoyment, self-confidence, interpersonal
bonding, lowering stress, and reproduction. Unlike a

porn model that defines sex as women's strength, illegal and perfect performance, and visual attention, it gives an intense and pleasurable feeling, which combines intimacy with exoticness, that is, the essence of healthy male sexuality.

Real-life intercourse is supportive and real, not ideal, perfect performance for your heart, emotions, or relationships. The most important lesson and also the most respectful one is to recognize that 5-15% of sexual experiences are unhealthy or dissatisfying to you or both of us. Can that be true indeed?

Comprehensively. Some people would never admit that it's valid for friends or their spouse, but it is.

Think Independently

Whether you are married, single, advanced, or a high school grader, in your 20's or 60's, we've all learned a key sexual lesson—"A real man never has sex questions or concerns. "Many people have a lesson opposite: "A real man is ready and capable of having sex with a woman at all times and in all locations." Not at all. Personal courage is required to confront the cultural messages that trap men in a competitive, perfect approach to sex.

Three out of four people hate a penis that is smaller than average. A surprising example. This reflects the business problem, except that it is statistically impossible. In culture, men lie and sit down together about sex, so there is an' feeding frenzy' about all sexual things— the number of partners you have had, the number of times you've had sex, the duration of your marriage, the number of orgasms you give your partner. You would never lose an erection, feel interested in sex, experience premature ejaculation or ejaculation or have questions or concerns about normal things. The control of this image and the blind exploitation of the blind transforms the true and stable male and gender.

Exercise 2.2: Enhancing Healthy Thinking and Confronting Poisonous Thinking

Men are not allowed to think about and talk about sex healthily. It tackles the pit. This workout. You are going to need confidence because we invite you to participate with men you know, admire, and trust in this small group debate. We recommend at least two more people and not more than seven. You could be the facilitator of the party. Two recommendations were proposed. First of all, try to make your attitudes, perceptions, and feelings as truthful, transparent, and descriptive as possible! Firstly, no bumpy, praiseworthy stories and no downs from other members of the group or from women.

Here are a few suggested topics: What did you learn about your childhood sex?

Who spoke to you? Who spoke?

How did you learn? What did you learn? Where did you receive gender details if no one spoke to you?

What is your best, most positive sex education experience, whether it be from family, college, church, or friends?

When was orgasm/ejaculation the first time? Emission of the night-time (wet dream), masturbation, sex, or other kids' fooling?? Was the experience optimistic or anxious?

How did you hear of marital sex for the first time? Have you been pleased and repelled?

What was your first porn contact— playboys, web videos, or sex stories? Was it fun, depressing, sexy, or culpable?

How old were you when you were your first partner? Was it a girlfriend, a prostitute, hook-up? Were there sex, rubbing, or intercourse, whether manually or orally? Was the experience good or bad?

Why did you act on the negative sexual encounters–an STD contract, a pregnant woman, sexual abuse, sexual abuse, termination, masturbation captured, ineffective first-time relationship?? Either you denied it, fabricated it, or nobody told it? Looking back, how have you sexually influenced this traumatic experience(s)?

What was your most positive sexual experience before your marriage?

What were the partnership value and sex quality? What were your most important results about yourself, women, and gender from this relationship?

What was your pre-marital encounter most negative? When long has it been, and how has it gone? Is there a legacy from this experience that distorts your sexual life as far as self-esteem, women's view, sexual vision, or relationships are concerned?

When was your relationship experiencing the most important and satisfying sex? What was it worth most to you? What can you do to revitalize sex in your marriage if this is different now?

What are your male friends ' questions to help you better understand yourself and your sexuality? Issues or concerns regarding gender, women, and relationships are particularly important today.

While you and your friends participate in this conversation, remain focused in a useful, truthful, and cooperative manner, not on rivalry or putdowns, on sharing information, attitudes, expertise or experiences. Knowledge is power. Knowledge is power.

Traditionally, people have no cooperative or constructive exchange of knowledge or experience. Ideally, this exercise will motivate you to do so and provide a basis for positive thinking about male sexuality.

What if this exercise can't be done? If it's more than you can organize this exercise, ask yourself some questions regarding your learning: how do you stop this conversation from happening? Do you not think you've got buddies with which you can trust? If you are honest, are you afraid of rejection? Were you straight with your sexual thoughts or past?

How to boost other than this men's party exercise your sexual health? Could you answer your personal magazine's 11 questions? Would you share your background, emotions, and learning with your partner openly?

Ten Things Men Need to Know about Their Individual Sexual Health

1. Treasure the five functions of sex in your Life

The more conscious you are, the better as a sex man. Five key motives (reasons) of gender are found in (table 2.2). These vary (for you and your partner) depending on your state of life and priorities.

Table 2.2: The Prime Reasons for Sex

1. Reduces tension to deal with the challenges of living a shared life.
2. It deepens and strengthens the intimacy and satisfaction that couples enjoy in a relationship.
3. It strengthens confidence and self-esteem.
4. It gives couples shared enjoyment and pleasure.
5. The default, biological function of procreation.

All five objectives may be relevant for you and your relationship at different times. Sex has different roles and definitions and can also serve many purposes.

Pleasure, particularly in long-term relationships, is often the fundamental feature of gender. Sex strengthens and specializes in your relationship. You feel appreciated and wanted, which enhances confidence and self-esteem. Boosting self-esteem in new relationships plays a major role in gender. Intimacy and satisfaction with relationships are a core part of effective, ongoing relations. This most probably happens before (pleasure) or after (play) sex instead of during sex and orgasm. Presumably, the least thought about stress management is about healthy sex, but that's a misunderstanding. The core element of healthy male sexuality is sex as a shelter or port in a storm.

Other motives might be to revitalize an adolescent after a difficult time, to re-join after a fight, or to feel important and energized after a professional rejection. For gender, procreation is the biological function. Although sex is inherently intended for reproduction, it is not a requirement but an option. You don't have to conceive of a baby as an excuse for being sexual or as evidence of being a man.

2. Make sure that sexuality is a part of your personality

Sex is more than your cock, your intercourse, and your ejaculation. The strong, integral part of your identity is as a person with your attitudes, actions, and feelings. Most men act as if sex is not a single facet of their personalities, but an entirely split personality.

So if you're considerate and compassionate in other areas of your life, it's part of your sexual style. If you are an amusing man or an adventurous guy, your style can be a factor, as well. You can incorporate into your sexual person if you are a spiritual/religious man.

Integrate into your sexual life your personality.

3. Let your expectations regarding your bodily needs be positive and genuine

Men that have a practical approach to work, facilities, sports in other parts of their lives often do not translate the lessons into their sexual bodies. For example, the porn picture is 100% credible, hard as steel, and overnight, and has an enormous penis. Porn sex has nothing to do with reality; it's about fantasy. The secret to understanding and acceptance of your sexuality is that your sexual reaction is based on your sexual body's realistic expectations. Vascular, neurological, and hormonal are three physiological systems that most affect sexual response. Sex is primarily a vascular response that raises blood pressure to your penis and genitals. Sexual response

A primary lesson is to misinterpret your sexual health if anything interferes with your health. For many people, it interferes with your vascular system because of its motivator to stop smoking.

You have to treat your body in a healthy way, especially your penis.

Sexual influencing physical factors are exhaustion, bad health, alcohol abuse, and drug abuse, poor diets, obesity, cancer, medicinal effects, lack of good diabetic control, and a sedentary lifestyle.

4. Appreciate the relational aspect of sexuality and not view it as autonomous

Teenage males discover that they can act autonomously without anything from their partner (experience, desire, anticipation, and orgasm). During their 30s and beyond, this practice is not good for men, during particular for men in extreme, continuous intercourse. Healthy male sexuality is not an independent but social activity.

Sex does not occur in the void, but in a relationship– either romantic or sexual friendship. You refer to the "online" partner of your imagination, a past partner, or the potential future even if you are not currently in a relationship. Men and women generally want the same gender advantages— emotional relations and sexual satisfaction. Traditionally we do this in various ways.

Young men have an emotional connection by sex historically, whereas women also obey gender through emotional intimacy. Such approaches are complementary, not oppositional, contrary to the social idea of a battle between the sexes. Sexuality requires lust, gratification, and fulfillment for both men and women. You may share the enjoyment and enhanced pair fulfillment, romantic, and erotic mates.

   5. *Appreciate the liking and worth of the sensation of touch*

Are sex and orgasm the only focus?? They are strong advocates of gender and pleasure, but your sexuality is too limited and potentially prone to dysfunction if you only concentrate on this subject. Ultimately nothing wins out if sex is intimacy or nothing. Perfect sexual performance (sex on demand) stress is ultimately a poisonous characteristic that undermines healthy sexuality. A good example of that is that the demand for a partnership driven by female ovulation produces erectile dysfunction and suppressed sexual desire from four of the five people who need to follow a protocol on infertility. He sinks into the pit of anticipative panic, failed relationships, and growing frustration and uncertainty.

What's that, antidote? It has a cycle of affection, sense, playfulness, eroticism, and relationship (Figure 2.2). This is the cycle of touch. The focal point is to share a pleasant touch. Intercourse is best understood as a natural extension of the cycle of gratification. Instead of passing-failure approach to relationships, we prefer the term feature rather than quality because we want to stress the importance of the natural response to communication and fun.

6. *You need to be smart in how you express and regulate your sexuality*

Sex isn't a warrant; it's an option. It will improve your life and friendship. You want to share your sexuality. The traditional male obligation of "being prepared at any moment to have sex with any woman" or of "taking everything you can" is insane and harmful. It seems like heretics to say "no" to gender, but to save, integrated sexuality, you can't say "yes," unless you can say "no" to dangerous and harmful sex.

In addition to the obvious concerns of unwanted sexual reproduction, STD / HIV and illegal sexual practices such as exhibitionism and child sexual abuse, uncontrolled sexuality involves compellingly using sex to reduce anxiety or to demonstrate something to yourself or someone else (i.e. not masturbating for gratification or stress reduction but to stop work or relationship frustrations).

Recall, sex is a combination of gratification, acceptance, intimacy with partners, active relationships, and personal and related satisfaction. Gender is a positive, integral part of manhood, but it is not the concept of manhood or masculinity. Express your sexuality to boost self-esteem and relationship

7. *Be cautious of the three methods of sexual arousal and integrate them into your sex styles as a couple*

You (and your partner) will find the right combination of arousals, which will be of use to you in your relationship when you know that there are three sexual arousal types.

a) Partner engaging excitement,
b) Self-entrance excitement and
c) Role-enactment excitement is the three forms of excitement (peruse frequency).

Styles are characterized by sexual attention, relationship, physical stimulation, and sexual feelings and imagination, or romantic scenarios.

Partner communication anticipation depends on partner contact and visual motivation.

This is the kind of sex in films that have been seen before. This uses two sexual directives— the "give" concept of gratification, and the big aphrodisiac is an active, enthusiastic partner.

The human being is alive, and the eyes are open, genital stimulation is received and given, speaking and energies are spoken (erotic or romantic). The enthusiasm of each partner plays off the other.

Arousal of self-entrance focuses on calming the body and being sensitive to touch. He closes his eyes, becomes relaxed and excited, often relying on a repetitive, stylized touch to respond and excite.

Arousal of positions is internally focused— plays, variety, tests, impressibility. Eroticism, not affection or enjoyment, is the focus. The women wear sexy clothing, play with the role of "sexually rough" or "virgin-prostitution" and have sex in new and dangerous ways, and make use of sexual devices like vibrators or pornographic film.

Many people use all three thrilling forms, while others use only two. The most common pattern is an interaction and self-entertainment series of partners.

Consider your situation's sexual pleasure theme.

The Common Male Worry—Sexual Boredom

Learning these thrilling types will help you overcome a common male issue–sexual familiarity. You fear that you're going to get too acquainted with sex with the same partner and get excited. The fear is that sex will lead to sexual dysfunction if it becomes so repetitive, monotonous, dull, routine. Pornographic producers understand this terror, which is why mainstream magazines, such as Playboy and Penthouse, are not one-time publications but regular copies. People with this fear of boredom claim their partner excessive sexual diversity or resort to pornography or sexual activity.

The wrong thing is to feel that sexual excitement depends solely on variety and freshness. It shows that partner engagement awakening is overreliance. When a man knows that sexual interaction with his partner is simpler and more secure with sensual self-entrance and can be complemented by roles, his sexual frustration and dysfunction worries are eased. Healthy sexuality incorporates multiple sexual meanings with several thrilling forms.

8. Be an intimate team with your sexual partner and value them as a sexual friend

The emphasis on romantic sexuality is in a one-night stand or a paid sexual encounter, where intimacy can interfere with sexual response. Nevertheless, sex is part of an intimate relationship in a sexual partnership, serious relationship, or marriage. Sex occurs in the background of your actions in real life, including employment, parenthood, and conflict.

Men typically seek emotional intimacy and interaction through gender. Sexuality requires wish, anticipation, pleasure, and contentment for both men and women. Being an intimate group at least means that sex is not a dominance battle or a manipulative fight.

Ideally, this means having your partner as your intimate and sexy companion, who can play several good emotional and physical roles with touch and sexuality and share positive or dishonest interactions without fault.

9. *Make sure that your real-life and your sex life are intertwined*

When you age and evolve, your sex life changes. When you stay at your house, a 25-year-old young person alone, a 35-year-old male who wants to conceive his second son, a 45-year-old man who is burdened by guilt, a 55-year-old male with the last child in school, a 65-year-old new retired man, a 75-year-old male who strives to overcome and sustain the odds. The role and sense of sex are very different. The incorporation of different events into the development of love considers the multiple objectives of gender.

Sex can include the release of anxiety through orgasm, emotional health, love and intimacy, and the sharing of tranquility about the death of a parent. Sexuality is very significant in the life of a man.

10.   *Understand that it is better to settle for sex that is good enough rather than a mediocre one. It is more true, gratifying, and of high Quality*

We have devoted such a central concept to this whole section.

Men fear that they will somehow feminize the Good Enough Intercourse and mean that they are second to the strongest. What a joke. They conclude that the Good-Enough Sex model is the logically, scientifically, and personally the safe, free, and practical solution to male and couple sexuality. You're a sexual person; you're not a sexual machine. It is far easier to stick to the traditional male template of flawless intercourse performance physically, psychologically, and fairly accommodating sexual variation and versatility.

Closing Thoughts

It's important that the basic concepts based on current scientific findings and clinically relevant recommendations provide a solid basis for safe men's sexuality. Most of these recent findings disagree with the traditional role of macho gender and high-performance standards. A smart, trusty, and strong sexual man requires knowledge of healthy sexuality between men (and couples) and optimistic, rational sexual expectations. As a man, you want to know and follow sound thinking for good sexuality.

Chapter 7: Positions to Try out

It's enticing to take off your clothing and go to it when you have strong sexual interaction with someone. But it is a great pleasure to take time to sample the encounter. "You can feel more relaxed, linked, and stimulated if you involve your body and mind in your sleep, both resulting in better sex," said Dr. Logan Levkoff, a professional instructor in the area of sexuality. You can also avoid the risk of making sex with the same series of assumptions, the same place, the same result by taking your time and being imaginative. This chapter aims to bring you some thoughts with which to play in the bedroom and new positions that you may not have tried and small changes and touches, which will offer you more pleasure. Nonetheless, new positions won't mean great sex. To make this evening perfect, use those tips to make your love more alive.

Before Sex

Before Love, fire a hot message at him in the afternoon, "What will you do later with me? According to Ian Kerner, Ph.D., "the writing process activates the mind in respects not seen in other tactile outlets." I've never been willing to see who will read the work clothes. "(See if you don't compose anything too explicit— you never know who may end up reading it). You are required to write in the blanks or build your visuals. The fusion of the writer's words with the recipient's meaning is a sort of gender itself. "Sometimes, you can have him in mind all day long, asking him what you are doing for that night.

To be motivated, you need to turn off your amygdala, which regulates fear and anxiety. So take a steamy bath about an hour before you prepare, soothe your brain and wake up your nerves. The hot water temperature can carry your skin's blood to render your entire body contact responsive.

During Sex

Slow gender is an essential component of sexual foreplay. Continue to pause at the core to explore, express an erotic dream, and swap massages. Begin with a sensible touch— a variety of activities designed to increase morale and enthusiasm without touching the genitals of each other. "The purpose is to relax and to establish affection," says Arlene Goldman, a licensed psychologist and sex therapist, Ph.D., Secrets of Sexual Ecstasy coauthor. Happy to have a relationship?

Choose a place to look into the eyes of each other, like priests or children, sitting up facing you. Check the 15 warm movements on the pages below; 15 more are to be discovered by flipping over the text. "Positions that give you a complete picture of each other's naked bodies may produce arousals so soon, while those that make eye contact improve familiarity and tend to make the anticipation more slowly," Levkoff says. Begin to move gradually across chaotic, circular patterns instead of quickly driving, without building up the constant force that induces instantaneous orgasm. Then continue to change different positions-the short break persists. But here's the vital thing to know about trying new sex positions: "The people can transform themselves into the most inventive sexual positions, but if they don't feel relaxed, pleasure-free and happy at the time, they certainly don't think the sex feels great," says Dr. Debbie Herbenick.

The woman at the top

The Cowgirl

Women on top Good for relaxation of G-spot.

The location of the female on the top helps you to see and experience variously and offers the psychological advantage of the speed and extent of penetration —

quick and intense thrust alternates. The sex therapist Rebecca Rosenblat has written about Seducing Your Man:' Shallow can raise the front fifth, which is the more responsive of your vagina.

Attempt this: Lie on your stomach and stretch your legs on top of your head.

Put your feet on top of his foot and move them to achieve a rocking motion that rubs your vulva and the clitoral region more pleasurably against his pubic bone.

Hot Trick –She shows you the V-stroke: draw a V with one hand index and ring finger and put her hands on her penis between each side of the clitoris. Drill your nails in a moving motion.

Hot tip—When you stimulate her manually or orally until she is extremely excited, it's simpler to climax her. Let her squat on the head from the woman-on-top role to motivate her orally.

Waterfall (a.k.a. head rush) Run to the side of your bed and put it back on the floor with your head and shoulders. When the blood reaches its peak, it produces psychological emotion.

Reverse Cowgirl a.k.a. Rodeo Drive

, halfway around the planet, gets a fantastic view from the rear with a cushion under his neck. The penetration depth and speed can be managed.

Having his arms spread out and flat on his side. Place your arms next to him, extend them out, straddle your knees with your foot facing him. Kneel, lower on yourself, and start riding up and down on your cock.

Then do this: Lean back and up to add pleasure and adjust the position of your penis inside you.

The Pole Hot Tip — You can easily reach yourselves from this location to stimulate and guide your penis to the best place to think.

Thighmaster benefits: you are doubly stimulated; you have an excellent view of your back and vagina.

Lay down on the back of your man, bent one of his legs, and leave the other out. Straddle the elevated leg and rotate it on each arm, so that your ass is in front of you. Hold your knee up, and you sit back and use it as help.

Place your vulva on to its top rubbing as the sensation decides before you reach orgasm.

You can rub your raised leg during the game from the Pole position. And cover his perineum to reach down. Look back to see the sexual gesture love him.

The love seat, guy chair advantages: better G-spot enhancement.

Seated

The love seat

Ask him to lie with his feet on the ground on the edge of the bed or a table.

Sitting between his arms, turn back on him and shut off. You can move the chair arms and click your legs. You can ride it back and forth. Through arching your back and grinding your buttocks into its crotch, track the entrance position. The hot Seat put you in the driver's seat while the doggy-style is about its supremacy.

Now do this: get into the base of your cock, scrotum, and perineum with your hand. Tell him to touch and raise the breasts in the meantime.

Take it Out of the Swiss Ball Flash Bedroom #1 Have a ball in your training area: use a stability ball to rebound the hot seat.

Position yourselves on top of a device mounted on the fastest hurry stage. VARIATION #2 Spin Cycle

VARIATION #3 The Heaven staircase offers proper seating and handrail for extra raising and support.

The Lap Dance

Lets you appreciate the security of yourself; relaxing for long meetings.

Tell him to lie on the bedside or table. Wrap your arms in front of him, climb over him, and sit on his lap. You can ride up and down on your penis when you press your legs or knees once you're on the saddle. Would you like to go quicker? Tell him to support him catch the feet to raise and bounce.

Do it now: lie on the rocking chair astride. Views with good vibes are made from old wooden rockers on hardwood and stone surfaces.

Sweet Tip — Ask him to kiss your nipples and let them explore your arms. This is the place to promote erogenous upper body, chest, neck, and face areas with plenty of imagination.

The Lazy Man, a.k.a. the Squat Thrust:

You are in charge, personal.

Place pillows behind his back and put his legs on the floor.

His knees straddle, the foot on the floor. Bend your knees to bend to him and bring your penis in with one arm. You can raise and rise on his shaft slowly or quickly if you want by pulling on your footballs and removing it.

Hot Tip–Think of your penis as a masturbator device to massage something and raise your clitoris. Tracey Cox, writer of Tracey Cox Kama Sutra Side by Side Spoon: a very personal face-to-face role that encourages appetite and hugging.

Side by Side

Spoon Facing a.k.a Sidewinder

This is an ideal position if you are pregnant or you have a knee injury, as it keeps the weight away from your body. Start to lay on your sides and face each other to get into this place. Open the legs a little so that it can penetrate you, so cover the arms so that you can lean against the clitoris on the section of your shaft outside of you. This casual face-to-face role is comfortable to touch.

Now attempt this: as thrusting in this posture is more complicated, use several strategies for additional relaxation such as scraping, rotating, or up and down movement.

Warm Tip: Hugs yourself 20 seconds before you get active. Hugging elevates the oxytocin levels, which produce a bonding compound, which will strengthen the connection.

Gift Wrap

Both of you are facing each other on your sides. Bend your hands, stick them entirely, and make your pussy into him. To join you, he'll put his legs between yours. Tie your arms across the neck. Wrap your feet.

Do this now: use your legs and feet for better penetration of force.

Scissoring benefits: provides a natural link to more imaginative roles. Spork a.k.a. Spoon and Fork Combo.

Lift your right leg when you lay on your back so that it is positioned 90 degrees between your legs and insert you. The tines of a spork, a spoon-and-fork utensil, will be the people. You can do this to avoid him or to ignore him.

Do this now: Raise your left leg if you are limber to increase the penetration range.

Hot tip — You could take your top leg from the spork position and put it on your back. With your fingertips, the clitoris can be quickly stimulated from here while it is inside.

Spoon and fork combo, a.k.a. spork
Go to a comfortable place if you're pregnant or if it's hot. Great for lengthy lovemaking as well. Nice one afterward to fall asleep.

You both lie down in the same position on your hands behind you. Bend your knees and turn your back to him to make your pussy easier to access. The width of your body modification shifts the direction of penetration, which allows you to rock and move.

Start it now: coordinate the movements. Now start. They follow one, and the other response to inhaling and exhaling simultaneously. The orchestrated tempo unlocks an unspeakable love conversation.

Hot Tip —To make her feel bigger, lean from the spoon posture, and lift her face to her breasts. Change your place to be above her top hip rather than behind her.

Go to Toe The Spider, a.k.a. The advantages of the Crab Walk: when staring at the game, the ears are still kept in contact.

Head to Toe

The Spider, a.k.a. The Crab Walk

We are both lying on the bed with feet facing each other, hands away protecting each other. Then switch onto his cock and carry on. Your thighs are squeezed around his long arms, his elbows dipping, and his feet flat on his pillow beyond his shoulders. Roll up and down then.

Do this now! Take your hands and sit as he lies down. Or he can sit upright and drag you into Lazy Man's position against his head.

Hot tip — Hers Help him turn you on as he massages you. Let him straddle your butt with your back massage. While his period wiggles, snuggle, and push your mons pubis onto the sheets in a rotating motion to activate your clitoris.

The fusion

The Spider's fusion raises your arms onto your back to maximize the muscle pressure in the course of the orgasm. It is harder to push and pound in circles by lifting the ass of the pillow.

Snow Angel a.k.a. Bottom's Up

This is difficult: lie on your back and have him place up in front of you.

Lift your arms, loop them around your back so he can get into your pelvis. Bring his rear to move up and down and support him. Fill your hands with a little relaxation motion.

Do this now: make him turn around to meet you when struggling to stay put. Change roles to face up this time to you.

Hot tip — You have easy access to your testicles from this location. Drag the hand gently to imagine his perineum between his testicles and anus.

Crisscross or the X Position

Long slow sex to create anticipation. Shallow thrusts strengthen the penile head's nerve endings.

Sit on the mattress with your feet in front of each other. Lift your left-right knee, then raise your right leg off your left leg. Go with him so that he can go back. You are both lying down, and the hands are an X. Slow, slow, long movements replace thrusting.

Do this now: reach back, hold your hands, and draw together.

Instead, take turns and sit back and lie without altering the tempo.

Empty the thoughts about the problems of the day by fantasizing about pleasant feelings.

Imagine an intimate encounter with your girlfriend or someone else when masturbating and pre-playing. Do not filter your feelings. Do not restrict your emotions. Wake up to your libido and anticipation completely open.

Oral

The Bees Knees

Good for out of home fellatio.

Behind him, kneel. Protect your lips and encircle your mouth around its glans. Piston the lips gradually, shifting velocities on his shaft up and down. He looks up at him from time to time. Feeling happy and pleasurable is a great joy. Stop moving your tongue across the mouth. Be vigilant with your lips, although for some people, light is sometimes lovely to wake up on the less alert shaft.

Do it now, put a dressing mirror on the side of his body against a window so that he can enjoy the view from the face downwards.

Hot tip — Hers Do not forget his family. Hot tip. Bring one of his testes to your mouth as you massage his shaft with your hand to make a combination he considers highly sexual

Hot Tip — She applies some mint or fruit-flavored lube to your shaft if your mouth gets sore after a while. Semen taste and texture don't like many people. You might want to hold the penis across your breasts when it reaches its orgasm so that it can ejaculate in and out of your cleavage.

The Sitter Face A convenient place for you. To him, an intimate one. Rest your head behind a cushion, and straddle it with your hands. Through supporting the headboard and floor, he could help himself.

Oral Stimulation

Cowgirl 69 a.k.a. Inverted 69,

If you are at 69, you can raise and push your pelvis to track the strength of oral stimulation in your clitoris. From there, your finger spells can be easily worked on your perineum, the sensitive area just below your testicles. Seek the spot for him on edge, too.

Start it now: turn over in 69 spots on your hands. Instead, rub the butts of each other and lick them clean.

Cold Tip— Place on your bedside a cup of warm tea and an ice cube. Alternate the ice cube and the drink in your mouth while you give him oral sex.

A butterflhoverr a.k.a. The Face Sitter

y increasing or by pressing down, you may steer the location and force of his tongue toward you.

Place the hands between his face to straddle it. Place on a support wall or headboard. Use your hands to grip your breasts and smooth your vulva on top while he does his job.

Try now this: keep his tongue tight, press your clitoris against it, while your hips turn.

Hot Tip — Women are often concerned about their aroma, even if most of the guys like their fragrance. Rinse the toilet before you get crowded, relax your mind.

Anal sex

Despite the capacity for enjoyment and anticipation, whether it be faith, hygiene, or alleged discomfort for purposes or theories, anal intercourse is hard to deal with. So let's break a few myths and explore how to think about anal sex before you start a safe conversation about bringing anal sex into your house, so you can prepare to have a "backyard session."

Anal sex is gross. Anal sex is filthy. Although there is a room of germs, likely, given the physiology involved, "no traffic will happen in the pipe." An anal bath and enema may help alleviate the fears of a couple of individuals. It is also necessary to use condoms as frequently as possible and to prevent cross-contamination, given what you may have seen in pornographic films and magazines.

Anal sex is impaired. Anal. You can have anal sex as pain-free and fun— if not more— than another kind of gender by following five easy steps to help you relax. Anal sex, because you can get it, is one such part of

153

life that the axiom takes care of what you want. Those who say it will sting will likely be disappointed, and those who fall under the roof will probably be back for a few seconds.

Sexually, your rectum can cause severe permanent damage. Anal intercourse will not permanently damage the rectum if done safely and as an item on your sex list.

When a heterosexual man plays with his ass or asks his girlfriend to do so, he can be homosexual or anal. A heterosexual man can't make him homosexual any more than he would convert a banana into a monkey using his thumb, tongue, or trick of anal pleasure. Therefore, not all gay men take part in anal sex, and not everyone enjoys bananas. I'll encourage you all to reach into all parts of your body for everyone reading this book; maybe you'll have fun like you never had if you were to take the P-spot–your prostate–or get next to it. Trust millions of satisfied hets: Anal playing isn't heterosexual— just erotic.

Set the stage

if you speak about anal sex musically, the soundtrack should be the We Have All Time in the World by Louis Armstrong instead of Bumblebee's Flight by Rimsky-

Korsakov. Relax, for in those who wait, good things come. The five notes of anal intercourse are contact, trust, lubricant, breathing, and space. Each of them will optimize the backdoor happiness to you and your family. If you're all gone, you can do the main thing about the pleasure of anal sex: RELAX.

The bedroom is the sexual location for this section, preserving and building on knowledge and trust— the two elements that should be present in every sexual relationship.

Take time to make it as easy and worry-free as possible for your bed and your friend. If the penetrated companion distracts and, worst, stupid, he may stop the anal encounter and keep him from returning to a stress-free state.

You should also take the time before starting to wash inside and outside.

When it's "the evening" today, indulge in quickly whatever, that is to suggest, an anal bath or an enema. Anal sex fans are also active in the cleaning process, which contributes to the excitement. Online or from any pharmacy store, you could purchase enamel bags or glasses.

Warmup: Rub Them the Right Way for Trust and Relaxation

In addition to being necessary for anal sex, the five elements that are required for pleasurable intimacy (communication, trust, lubricants, breathing, time) form an integral part of the traditional tradition of sensuality: massage. Your companion could tell a whole love story with the gentle and caring laying of hands. A massage always stabilizes and calms our body. Because massages are intended to ease us, time and flexibility are needed–a lesson which is also essential for the enjoyment of anal intercourse.

Our hair, rectal flakes, and one of the most excellent all-natural massage lubricants is my favorite sex lubricant: organic coconut oil. Stable at room temperature — "love butter" —and prepared to melt in or on, coconut oil has a tropical-revival scent, and after that movie, it could become your second favorite in your house. The cocoa oil should be scooped into two saucers: one for the pre-game treatment and one for a "main event." Do not scoop directly from the original container for hygienic reasons.

Full-body massages are excellent, but three factors are the better in this example for a backside, the only massage. First of all, she will be met by the starting position of gender, and therefore we do not aim for the massage to establish intimacy.

Additionally, his sexual thoughts won't be gynocentric as his breasts and vulva remain hidden as she lays on her stomach. Second, the end is in sight with her rear-facing up and right before it. Particularly first face-up massages will lead many to be anxious, as everyone should be calm and ready for what to do. All their vital organs are revealed.

During the treatment, he will take time to realize what his respiration can do by watching and sensing his back rising or sinking beneath his feet. He could straddle her legs with the head facing her to move her back and up, when she exhales, and then encourage her feet, as she inhales, to float gently back to their starting point. He could then massage her arms, thighs, hands, palms, neck, and again to stay as far as practicable from her pussy, partly to make awareness that he is headed straight into Anal Sex, and partly to stop her from dreaming. Be vigilant when massaging her, that she does not tickle; this tightens the hole where she wishes you can relax. Another successful and affectionate way to help her calm is to always put another hand on her because she is face-down and cannot see what he is doing.

He will focus on soothing her and building confidence. It must hold its hands away from the valley between its muscles of two butts until it is prepared for the next step. It might be a smooth, realistic signal to draw a knee towards you or underneath it, showing your fingerprint to your rose.

At the moment, he should not enter her; however, she welcomes him to touch her bottom. He should instead lubricate his fingers with another coconut oil saucer, which can then end the penetration. She could lay flat and float under her navel a little pillow to raise her rear.

Using his oiled fingertips, he could move his anus around and place light pressure on one of his minor fingers to reach the gap. So, he should not try to get into her as much as she wishes. She is in full control. It works when she reaches out to the rectum as if trying to pull in her hand. To loosen the first sphincter wider. This phase of anal stimulation gives you the opportunity to inject a large quantity of lubricant into the penetrated region. He can put a finger just up to one knuckle and tug and move it so gently while he stays in a method that sounds great to all sensitive newcomers. The game can be used to improve spouse and single-sex. I name the game "Tug of Wow."

When she starts calming, even with two fingers in advance, he could switch to a different and similarly well-liked finger and his acceptance. The pair are ready for the next step if they are comfortable, lubricated, and relaxed and know how to regulate the strength of their breath and penetration.

Although this might seem to the penetrator a lot of time, the penetrated individual does need it. If the roles were reversed — a female could enter a person with fingertips or toys (some people call it a street lingo)—men would have empirical evidence that those five measures were necessary for interaction, confidence, respiration, lubricant, and time relaxation. And, ladies, if your partner tells me what a competent and compassionate anal lover you're dating, then I hope that she will be tied with you.

She should feel in control to make a person relax during anal sex. One of the easiest ways to accommodate her penis–and one of the best ways to position her rectum to match her cock–is to get her hands on top of her.

It helps her to monitor penetration depth and pace, and she can get off quickly every time. Very often, when the man's back draws momentum towards his chest, glutes and arms, the blood that must be in his penis. She should be enough to compensate by wrapping her sphincter across her dick, moving away, and relaxing the anal grasp once she lowers onto him.

With anal sex, I urge clients to have antibacterial wipes at hand, and this is the perfect time for them to disinfect their hands while they step backward. The first place goes on with the trust the pair have built up until now, which helps the female to control the penetration depth and speed. It also makes communication between the brain and the ear.

Lie on your back, on a cushion with your face. Stroke yourself as she mounts you to protect your hardon.

Straddle his thighs, toward his mouth. A solution is to put your feet down on either side of his legs if your knees can cope with the pair. You must use your hands for protection if you choose to take this gymnastic pose, or you risk sitting on his penis to wipe away the leverage provided in this position. His cock can easily pass through the first sphincter and avoid the second. If so, take a deep breath in and move your rectum and on his cock while you are exhaling. Hold this place, if possible, before you feel free. This is an "established" stage of penetration of the anal-penile.

Only keep steady before she tells you to drive things further. As much as you like porn –film anal sex, it is a relaxation test. And seek to get also into her pussy rather than deeper into her brain. Is it great for her, and what is it that she thinks and feels? Sometimes, share your feelings with her. Is that a turn-over, or are her skyscraping a nutcracker for her ass?? Note that for any side, anal sex ought not to be uncomfortable.

You can stimulate your nipples or your own if you don't hold onto one or both of his hands. Tell him what he must-do if you feel comfortable and want to give up any orgasmic control over him. Often, you can grow to command or even stop penetration on your knees and feet. You let him drive less into you by bending back.

Once, ask how shallow or how broad must his gestures be. Most women come through anal penetration in tandem with the mouth or clitoris brushing against their pubic bone. Love the rush and come to this place as often as you want.

Since many men find Anal Sex to be more robust than masturbation, they might have to complain that their boa strategy is delayed and lightened. You hazard ejaculation otherwise, and your job as a human dildo will be abandoned. Return to the first section to read about gender masturbating practice, should you start to ejaculate early during anal sex.

The pair will step on to the next role when she feels ready for more action and decides to go on.

Transition

I don't recommend the roll-over transfers often seen in porn films or used for vaginal intercourse, because they can end in a penile fracture. Both of you are better off disengaging, changing positions or reappearing, and planning for reentry. Now, before you let him back in your harbor, lets out his dingy safely.

Lift far enough to exit your butt with your dick gradually.

Sit on it, lift the head, and touch it. Hold on.

Turn on your side and lie on the mattress next to your head. And turn on your back for the rest of the way. Comfort the lower back with a large cushion to keep it as comfortable as possible. If you are new to anal sex, have a weak core muscle group, or have a pain in your chest, this global aid is critical; but you'll get nestled in your back too.

Turn your back to her and draw your legs into your body to cover your knees and back.

Push up on the two arms and roll over, so you now have your face over your pillow, so your neck and hers, in the same way, is "doggy-like."

Shift your hands back up to your knees; from your friend who is expecting you, you should be a couple of feet on his foot. Slide your legs forward so that both of you are in line.

Sprinkle your hands in the pleasure soup— not the relaxation soap — then take your butt and cock-up. Place your legs in the neck, which raises your pelvis-just like the thin coil under your leg.

Taking her thighs in every hand and bring her on your bent knees— the ramp— as you once more place your dick on your butt. Now you are ready to enjoy it!

The Ramp

Because she was in a driver's seat for anal sex, in this changed missionary position, her mind and body are in a spot where she can transfer her love to the next point. His knees, creating the' ramp,' protect his buttocks and lower back in this role and stop him from producing jarring and aggressive thrusts, which he could be tempted to do in the back.

Be vigilant to move to her as it might have constricted one or both of her anal sphincters. If it gets too close, go back to digital penetration gradually and love until it relaxes.

After you have achieved it through her secondary love stream keys, switch the palm on your forearms and place the bent legs on either side of your neck on her hands.

You have the hands now at your side, the elbows on your side or at the corners of your arms, your upper back on your stomach, and the vulva pointing up to your navel. It is also a period for playing with your vulva or clitoris or of putting a vibrator on your clit, nose, vulva, and vagina.

The penetration of your hips and legs can create global by gripping them. Both can take small, rocking movements to make short or deep strokes that are slow or strong.

Conclusion

Thank you for making it through to the end of the book Sex Positions Guide, let's hope it was informative and able to provide you with all of the necessary information you may need to make sure that you have a healthy, intimate and satisfying sex life to cherish with your partner.

The next step is to make use of the information and tools you have read in this book to make sure you have an improved sex life.

- If you are in a relationship, communicate more with your partner regarding what you are and are not comfortable with, talk to each other about your fetishes, and maybe try them out once in a while to further strengthen your bond as a couple.
- Always remember that sex is a mutually beneficial activity in a relationship. You, therefore, need to always treat your partner as an equal in the game (unless you have both agreed to explore submissive fetishes).
- When it comes to the use of sex toys, sexual lubricants, and gels, every product has different

reactions, depending on the person's body. When it gets to a point where you have decided to introduce such elements in your sex lives, also make it a point of acquiring them together to find products that both of you are comfortable in using.

- Make it a point of going through the book once in a while with your partner to make sure you are always on top of your game in having a healthy, satisfying, and productive sex life.

Finally, if you found this book useful in any way, a review on Amazon is always appreciated!

Printed in the USA
CPSIA information can be obtained
at www.ICGtesting.com
LVHW020757260923
759121LV00074B/776